Experiencing Hildegard

Experiencing Hildegard

Jungian Perspectives

Avis Clendenen

CHIRON PUBLICATIONS ❖ WILMETTE, ILLINOIS

I am the rain
coming from the dew
that causes the grasses
to laugh with the joy of life.

—Hildegard (adapted by Nancy Fierro from the *Symphonia*)

Dew is, figuratively, anything that falls lightly and in a refreshing manner, an emblem of morning or fresh vigor, something like such drops of moisture, as in purity, delicacy, or refreshing quality. The dewdrop on the blade of grass was one of Hildegard's favorite metaphors for the conception of Christ. In Hildegard's hymn to Mary, "O viridissima virga" (O greenest twig), she sings:

Your womb held joy like the grass
When the dew falls, when heaven
freshens its green—
even as it did in you,
O mother of all gladness.

(*Sister Wisdom*, pp. 169–170)

Dew is emblematic of the ever available grace of the gifting, greening Spirit of God, who refreshes and invigorates like dew upon the grass.

Book and cover design by Marianne Jankowski.
Printed in the United States of America.

Library of Congress Cataloging-in-Publication Data

Clendenen, Avis.
  Experiencing Hildegard : Jungian perspectives / Avis Clendenen.
    p. cm.
  Includes bibliographical references and index.
  ISBN 978-1-888602-44-9 (alk. paper)
1. Hildegard, Saint, 1098-1179. 2. Jungian psychology. I. Title.

BX4700.H5C54 2009
282.092—dc22
                                        2009004769

Passages from Jung, C. G., *The Collected Works of C. G. Jung* © Princeton University Press reprinted by permission of Princeton University Press.

"God of our Daily Drudge" (page 56), in *Karl Rahner: Spiritual Writers,* edited by Philip Endean and published by Orbis Books 2004, pp. 49-50. Reprinted by permission from Orbis Books.

"Praying" (page 55) and "The Uses of Sorrow" (page 75) from *Thirst: Poems by Mary Oliver* (2006) reprinted by permission from Beacon Press.

For my mother
Margaret Ann Bailey Clendenen
1922–2001

Like Hildegard,
you did not live a small life

Jesus said, "If you bring forth that which is within you,
that which you bring forth will save you.
If you do not bring forth that which is within you,
that which you do not bring forth will destroy you."

The Gospel of Thomas, no. 70, 200 CE

You understand so little of what is around you
because you do not use what is within you.

Hildegard of Bingen
Scivias 1.2.29, 1141/2–1151/2 CE

We cannot understand a thing until
we have experienced it inwardly.

C. G. Jung, *Psychology and Alchemy,* par.15

Contents

I consider it my task and duty to educate my patients
and pupils to the point where they can accept the
direct demand that is made upon them from within.
This path is so difficult that I cannot see how the
indispensable sufferings along the way could be
supplanted by any kind of technical procedure.
Through my study of the early Christian writings
I have gained a deep and indelible impression of
how dreadfully serious an experience of God is.
It will be no different today.

Carl G. Jung
Letters, vol. 1
26 May 1923

Acknowledgments

My head is full of dew...

—Canticle of Canticles 5.2

The Canticle of Canticles or Song of Songs falls into the category of wisdom literature. The sacred book is a collection of love poetry: poems of yearning, joy, weariness, admiration, and the savoring of deep memory. I have known these feelings intimately over the past few years as this book ripened into print and picture. The six simple words from the Canticle of Canticles capture my experience in preparing these final words for *Experiencing Hildegard: Jungian Perspectives.*

My head is full of the dew of gratitude to Barbara Howard and the Howard Family Foundation, whose generosity is seemingly boundless in support of the Sister Irene Dugan, r.c., Legacy Project. This book joins *Spirituality in Depth* (2002) and *Love Is All Around in Disguise: Meditations for Spiritual Seekers* (2004) as the final book in the trilogy that completes the Dugan Legacy Project, and I thank Barbara for her commitment to my efforts to preserve and perpetuate Sister Irene's unique spiritual vision.

I wish to thank former student Kevin Loftus and Sisters of Mercy Marie Fox and Martin dePorres Smukowski for their generous support.

Murray Stein, Chiron Publications general partner, has been stalwart in his efforts to bring to print the texts associated with the Dugan Legacy Project. I thank Murray also for connecting me to Dr. John Dourley, who provided the seven references to Hildegard in Jung's *Collected Works.* Their guidance in my pursuit to find Hildegard in Jung has been invaluable.

My head is so full of dew when I think of the immediate affirming responses I received when I asked Therese Schroeder-Sheker, Carmen Acevedo Butcher, Gabriele Uhlein, OSF, David Richo, and John Dourley to read the manuscript and offer comments. Their insights helped to green the text and their words of encouragement eased my anxieties about the merit of the work. I have such admiration for their accomplishments.

Noreen Sullivan, library technician at Byrne Memorial Library of Saint Xavier University in Chicago, offered far more than technical support. I never lacked for a companion with whom to commiserate and who believed that every request for yet another volume of Jung's *Collected Works* was worth the effort.

Dr. Kathleen Alaimo, Dean of the College of Arts and Sciences, Saint Xavier University, celebrated the Howard Family Foundation awards and enthusiastically assisted me in constructing the funded appointment as the Sister Irene Dugan Scholar in Spirituality. Every teacher-scholar should be so lucky to have such a dean.

Saint Xavier University colleagues Jan Bickel and Martha Morris worked with me to bring "Hildegard of Bingen: The Music of Her Visions" to living performance in 1996 and 2007. Dr. Bickel's artistic leadership pressed our students to new vocal heights and depths, leaving them and the audiences stunned by the beauty.

My colleague and friend, Dr. Brian Klug, Senior Research Fellow in Philosophy at St. Benet's Hall in Oxford, has been a muse of understated inspiration, challenging me to the more of the profession.

My head is full of dew when I consider how grateful I am for the prodding of Dr. Pozzi Escot, President of the International Society of Hildegard von Bingen Studies, who insisted I present my findings on Hildegard in Jung at the 25th Anniversary Conference of the International Society of Hildegard von Bingen Studies in May 2008. Creating and delivering that presentation solidified my commitment to finish the book, and I am indebted to her for the telephone calls in which she would not take no for an answer.

Dyane Sherwood, editor of *Jung Journal: Culture and Psyche*, was exceedingly instructive in working with me on the article that became a précis for the book. Susan Harris, managing editor of Words Without Borders, worked with me for a year in organizing the material, editing various chapters, offering creative solutions, and never failing to be generous with her talent and time. Siobhan Drummond, Chiron editor and wordsmith extraordinaire, brought a precision of expression and artistic design to the whole project. She is dew upon any work of words struggling to come alive on the page. I thank designer Marianne Jankowski for the artful blend of the contemporary and medieval in the look of the book.

Many years ago, someone in a public lecture asked me who inhabited the spirit of Hildegard today, and I named Sister Joan Chittister, OSB. Unbeknownst to me, in the audience that day was a friend of hers, Sister Mary Benet McKinney, OSB, who took the time to read the manuscript and introduce me to Sister Joan Chittister, OSB. I shall never forget this kindness. The Hildegard quote below is my tribute to Sister Joan and the many women of dangerous memory.

Last, my head is so full of dew when I savor the deep memory of my mother and the joy the publication of this book would have brought to her. Because of these and so many others, I find not only my head but also my heart is full of dew.

Avis Clendenen
27 January 2009

Who are the prophets?
They are a royal people,
who penetrate mystery
and see with the spirit's eyes.

In illuminating darkness they speak out.

They are living, penetrating clarity.
They are a blossom blooming only
on the shoot that is rooted in the
flood of light.

—Hildegard, from Gabriele Uhlein,
Meditations with Hildegard of Bingen, p. 126

Introduction

The originality of a woman's work might never have been recorded.
If recorded, it may not have been preserved.
If preserved, it may have remained submerged or not translated.
If translated or available, it might not be included in the curriculum.
If included in the curriculum, it might not be examined as worthy of critical attention.
And therefore, not taken seriously.

—Rosemary Radford Ruether (1988)

In the context of Western patriarchy women have been marginalized again and again to the edges of history and out of collective consciousness. Women of talent existed and pioneered new vistas of thought and practice—and then they were forgotten. Thus, the women coming after them—women through time—had to start all over again, repeating the process in order to regain the knowledge lost. While Hildegard achieved fame in her own time, she was almost lost to history. This is precisely why we need *another* book on Hildegard.

Even more important, women have for millennia
been forced to prove to themselves
and to others their capacity for full humanity and
their capacity for abstract thought . . .

Why have there been no great female intellectual
innovators? I believe there have been such women
and we have not sufficiently respected them
in the narrative of the past.

—Gerda Lerner, *The Creation of Feminist Consciousness*

1

A brief pause to consider theologian Rosemary Ruether's steps of female invisibility reminds us of the continued importance of taking women seriously. It wasn't until 1993 that historian Gerda Lerner completed *The Creation of Feminist Consciousness: From the Middle Ages to Eighteen-seventy*, the companion volume to *The Creation of Patriarchy* (1986). Interestingly, the dust jacket for *The Creation of Feminist Consciousness* displays Hildegard of Bingen's self-portrait from an illuminated medieval manuscript and is adjacent to a photograph of Sojourner Truth (1797–1883). The juxtaposition of these visual images stimulate the viewer to take seriously the scores of women lost in time whose stories need telling not only for their sakes, but for our own.

> That man over there says that women need to be helped into carriages, and lifted over ditches, and to have the best place everywhere. Nobody ever helps me into carriages, or over mud-puddles, or gives me any best place! And ain't I a woman? Look at me! Look at my arm! I have ploughed and planted, and gathered into barns, and no man could head me! And ain't I a woman? I could work as much and eat as much as a man—when I could get it—and bear the lash as well! And ain't I a woman? I have borne thirteen children, and seen most all sold off to slavery, and when I cried out with my mother's grief, none but Jesus heard me! And ain't I a woman?
>
> —delivered by Sojourner Truth, Women's Convention in Akron, Ohio, 1851

But why then rely on Carl Jung for a theoretical framework from which to view Hildegard and her creative genius? The latter part of the twentieth century witnessed an international and interdisciplinary resurgence of interest in spirituality. Today a search on the World Wide Web for "Christian spirituality" yields three million sites (Dreyer and Burrows 2005, p. 363). Within the past few decades both scholarly and popular interest has focused on the connections between human development and spiritual growth, nurturing emotional and spiritual intelligence, the relationship between the cure of the body and the healing of the soul. While theology involves a conscious, intellectual exercise, spirituality extends beyond the conscious intellect into our unconscious or half-conscious depths (Carr 1988, p. 201). The more we are inundated with sound bites and superficial images, the more the human spirit hungers for quiet soundscapes and rich symbols. The integration of psychology and spirituality has its roots in the work of one of the founders of modern depth psychology, Carl Gustav Jung (1875–1961).

One letter among Jung's voluminous correspondence highlights the true focus of his life work when he writes, "the main interest of my work is not concerned with the treatment of neuroses, but rather with the approach to the numinous" (*Letters* 1, Aug. 20, 1945). Depth psychology attends to what lies beneath the surface of conscious awareness. From Jung's point of view the other psychologies of his time failed to address the psychic suffering that brought people to seek analysis in the first place. Jung was concerned with an increasingly fragmented Western culture and an unevolved Christian tradition. The symbols of the Christian tradition no longer captured the imagination of the modern person. Jung's belief about the potential demise of Christianity was not synonymous with a declining need for the life of religion. A new form of religious thought and practice was evolving, "and it was Jung's clear opinion and personal objective," according to Murray Stein, "that this would be a transformed version of Christianity, rather than an entirely new form of religion" (1985, p. 158).

Jung saw much emotional distress as the suffering of the soul that has yet to discover its meaning. He said, "all creativeness in the realm of the spirit as well as every psychic advance of man arises from the suffering of the soul, and the cause of the suffering is spiritual stagnation" (1932a, par. 497). Jung thought it safe to say that in more than thirty years of clinical practice every one of his clients suffered illness because of his or her dislocation from inner meaning; none of them healed apart from regaining a religious outlook on life (ibid., par. 509). "It was the task of modern depth psychology to forge the link that would rejoin modern men and women to their ancestral religions" (Stein 1985, p. 10). Jungian depth psychology is a sacred science that examines the ways unconscious processes in the human personality reveal themselves in symbol, dream, images, art, and various biological and emotional symptoms. Healing means reestablishing a connection with the transcendent, the numinous within, which, as Ann Ulanov says, paraphrasing Jung, "brings with it the ability get up and walk to our fate instead of being dragged there by a neurosis" (1999, p. 126).

Jung grappled with the failure of Christianity in modernity, the failure of its tradition, beliefs, symbols, and practices to hold meaning in the emotional and intellectual life of human beings in the modern era. It has been said that Hildegard's lush twelfth-century interior life foreshadowed twentieth-century Jungian insight into the rich contents of the unconscious in human personality. This book offers a synthesis of aspects of Hildegard's spirituality in fresh combination with insights from Jungian depth psychology, particularly that of the life of the unconscious and the reality of the soul. Murray Stein contends that Jung was guided in his writings by an unseen hand, a largely unconscious *spiritus rector* [guiding spirit]. This guiding spirit prompted his strong urge to heal Christianity, which led him unerringly to the very heart of the tradition's ailments and deepened his desire to offer it his psychotherapeutic help (Stein 1985, p. 17). In many ways, eight centuries earlier Hildegard was motivated by the same impulse and guided by a similar spirit, the *umbra viventis lucis*: the Living Light within her soul.

It is of note that the seven references to Hildegard's work are found in volumes 5, 9, 10, 11, 13, 14, and 18 of Jung's *Collected Works*. While his reliance upon her as an illustration of various points is not overwhelming by any means, the fact is that he makes note of her in seven different volumes of his work spanning decades of the development of his thinking. She is not a passing fancy but a figure present to him through the decades. This book examines these references and takes seriously Jung's interest in a woman from another era upon whom he could rely while pioneering the rich, colorful, symbolic spiritual terrain of the unconscious. Jung appreciated mystics and thinkers like Hildegard who corroborated his conviction that mysticism was rooted in archetypal imagery. Jung was fascinated enough by his knowledge of Hildegard of Bingen to use her interior discoveries to support some of his empirical findings. In *Alchemical Studies*, Jung comments that Hildegard of Bingen is "an outstanding personality quite apart from her mysticism" (1957, par. 42).

There are some important criticisms to note in approaching Hildegard's work through a Jungian lens. Jung's theories, such as that of the archetype, hold deep insight and can be granted too much ontological heft and misconstrued in such a way as to imagine that they are not embedded in reality that is socially constructed. Some Jungian theory can function to legitimate the status quo, reinforcing social roles, constricting growth, particularly for women. Jung has been criticized for his treatment of certain Christian doctrines, particularly his novel, near-heretical approaches to the transcendence and absolute goodness of God, the doctrine of the Trinity, and the positing of the shadow in divinity or the dark side of God. Certain of Jung's notions are interpreted as perpetuating sexual stereotypes and focusing far too much on the individual at the expense of social justice. Jung spoke of the ultimately unimportant events of world history because he believed that, in the last analysis, the essential thing is the life of the individual. Some have postured that Jung's efforts to "heal" Christianity are more reflective of his own unfinished business with the faith and struggle for self-coherence. Others postulate that Jung's vision of Christianity aims at a new religious consciousness that is as different as Christianity became from Judaism in that it transformed the later into something that contained and surpassed it. Such critiques will be recognized in developing the point of view this book offers.

Hildegard is most popularly known for the originality of the composition of her exquisite music, which will be described in the early chapters of this book. Hildegard's growing fame also centers on her best-known work, the *Scivias* (1141–52), her multimedia manuscript of twenty-six visions with theological commentary. More will be said of her various illuminations later, but it is interesting to note that the original twelfth-century illuminations that formed the core of her first work, the *Scivias*, existed until 1945. The original manuscript was taken to Dresden for protection from the bombing during the Second World War and has been missing ever since. However, during the late 1920s her nuns carefully hand-copied these originals, and today they are in the library of the Abbey of St.

Hildegard in Rudesheim, Germany, across the Rhine River from Bingen. They remain unavailable for public viewing, although two other illuminated manuscripts of the *Scivias* are available to the public in libraries in Lucca, Italy, and in Heidelberg, Germany.

> In our own day the voice that Hildegard called
> "a small sound of the trumpet from the living
> Light" is resounding once more . . . Hildegard
> unites vision with doctrine, religion with science,
> charismatic jubilation with prophetic indignation,
> and the longing for social order with the quest
> for social justice in ways that continue to challenge
> and inspire.
>
> —Barbara Newman, in Hart and Bishop, *Hildegard of Bingen*

This book seeks the middle ground between the more impersonal discourse of a scholarly examination of Hildegard through the lens of Jungian depth psychology and a purely popular appropriation of Hildegard and Jung for personal spiritual growth. This middle ground provides a serious read into Hildegard in her time and the opportunity to meet her in the context of our time, where interest in the integration of depth psychology with the practice of spirituality has been growing for many years. These relationships will be examined with attention to avoiding co-opting Hildegard's originality for an agenda that did not exist at her time. Thus, the scope of this book excludes a comprehensive exploration of the Christianity of her time and the critical examination of the theological import of all her visions, as well as any significant foray into her music. The book's appeal to a popular audience parallels the appeal Hildegard held for the populace in her time and is in fact integral to her identity. This indeed is the task of a pastoral theologian: to interpret the tradition and its sources with sensitivity and imagination, working to make the testimony of the past interesting, accessible, and meaningful to a contemporary audience. This is what I have attempted to do in the pages that follow.

The book relies heavily on secondary sources with respect to Hildegard's extraordinary range of multidisciplinary insights.

This reliance on secondary sources is purposeful. Others more skilled than myself have translated her complex and artistically lush thinking from the original Latin, the official written language for science, diplomacy, law, and everything related to church life, and from German, the vernacular of her culture. In addition, the secondary sources provide the reader further reliable sources in English to pursue.

I presuppose basic knowledge of analytical psychology, Christian theology, and Jungian terminology and perspectives that have become part of the general knowledge. The many followers of psychospiritual integration, as well as spiritual direction practitioners, religious professionals, and pastoral therapists, will be familiar with the concepts in this book, precisely because of the substantive insight into the dynamics of the human experience of the sacred provided by depth psychological theory.

The book does not pose a fundamentally new argument about Hildegard of Bingen's life and work but endeavors to make her insights and spirit accessible, particularly to those seeking a feminine muse on the spiritual journey. Each chapter explores a unique facet in the rich array of Hildegard's thought by exploring the theme in the context of her own time and in her own words, then relates Hildegard's particular point of view to insights from depth psychology. Finally, each chapter ends with an application section to prompt personal engagement in making connections to one's own experience and sharing conversation with others. Such exercises help us discern the workings of destructive and creative forces busy within and around us. Attending to psychospiritual insights and methods can lead to enlightenment, even transformation.

The invitations at the end of each chapter provide incentive for readers to explore the depths of their own life journeys and spiritual quests. In order fully to experience Hildegard, readers must be open to the unexplored. Keeping a journal as you read this book will bring you closer to Hildegard's own experience of releasing the truth held within by "putting her hand to writing." Keeping a private journal or notebook to record responses to the suggested guided exercises and meditations will assist you in deepening your experience of encounters with your own interior life. The act of "uncensored" writing bridges the inner and outer worlds in which we live. It creates an avenue of expression for the unconscious to emerge through the conscious activity of writing. There are only a few rules that govern journal writing (see Baldwin 1990):

* Your entries form a private document and belong exclusively to you; while you may choose to share your journal entries verbally with your spiritual mentor, no one should be given direct access to your writing.

* Your writing should flow freely without self-censure of any idea, thought, recollection, memory, or feeling.

* Date every entry.

* Avoid making any other rules.

Journaling, as Samara O'Shea says, guides you into speaking and speaking (writing and writing) until at last you hear yourself (2008, p. xv).

The process of writing is always a healing process
because the function of creation is always, *always*,
the alleviation of pain—the writer's first of all
and then the pain of those who read what she has written.
Imagination is compassionate. Writing is a form of
making, and making humanizes the world.

—Richard Rhodes, quoted in O'Shea, *Note to Self*, p. xx

These pages take Hildegard seriously. As an original. Recorded. Preserved. Translated. Taught and studied. The reader is invited to cross the threshold. Hildegard's voice echoes across time into this now:

Good People,
Most royal greening verdancy,
rooted in the sun,
you shine with radiant light.

In this circle of earthly existence
you shine
so finely,
it surpasses understanding.

God hugs you.
You are encircled
by the arms of the mystery of God.

   (from Gabriele Uhlein, OSF, *Meditations with*
   Hildegard of Bingen)

A Portrait of Hildegard of Bingen

Praise the lives you did not choose.
They will heal you, tell your story, fight
for you. You eat the bread of their labor.
You drink the wine of their joy . . .

Praise our choices, sisters, for each doorway
open to us was taken by squads of fighting
women who paid years of trouble and struggle,

who paid their wombs, their sleep, their lives
that we might walk through these gates upright.

—Marge Piercy, *Circles on the Water*

In the eleven hundredth year after the
Incarnation of Christ, the teaching
and fiery justice of the Apostles,
which Christ had established among
the Christians and spiritual people,
began to slow down and turn
into hesitation.
I was born in those times.

—Hildegard, *The Vita of Hildegard*

Introduction

By all rights, a woman like Hildegard of Bingen ought not to have existed, but she did. Hildegard, unlike countless other female thinkers, was *not* written out of history. The recorded and preserved originality of Hildegard's work led many in the latter part of the twentieth century and at the dawn of the twenty-first century to attend, seriously and critically, to her phenomenal multidisciplinary legacy. On the nine-hundredth anniversary of Hildegard's birth in 1998, Barbara Newman wrote the following:

> Hildegard is the only woman of her age to be accepted as an authoritative voice on Christian doctrine; the first woman who received express permission from a pope to write theological books; the only medieval woman who preached openly before mixed audiences of clergy and laity with full approval of church authority; the author of the first known morality play, and the only twelfth-century playwright who is not anonymous; the only composer of her era known both by name and by a large corpus of surviving music; the first scientific writer to discuss sexuality and gynecology from a female perspective; and the first saint whose official biography includes a first-person memoir. (1998, p. 1)

"God's little trumpet," as Hildegard referred to herself, was a remarkable woman by the standards of any time. During her own lifetime she was referred to as "Bingen's jewel," "Sybil of the Rhine," and "*prophetessa teutonica*." The range and depth of her work singled her out then and now. In her early forties, she became a "writing woman," thereby appealing to midlife women who struggle to bring their inner world of insight and truth to creative expression.

Hildegard's story reveals the dynamics of how one can success-fully negotiate the forces that submerge consciousness and creativity. She is a witness to the costly protest that the way things are need not remain that way forever. She exemplifies the breakthrough of female originality and ingenuity by creating new roles for herself and innovative avenues of expression, while remaining within the apparent confines of a patriarchal worldview. The modern images of "finding voice" and "giving voice" that have arisen within women's quest for greater liberation in the last part of the last century find a sister-companion in Hildegard, who, once eclipsed, emerges into contemporary consciousness.

The first half of this chapter places Hildegard in the context of her own turbulent time and explores, at some length, her multifaceted productivity. The second half identifies some of the defining moments in Hildegard's life and offers connections to' Jung's theories, which are developed in subsequent chapters. Last, the application at the end of the chapter invites readers to engage a still-living Hildegard and the truth that her history, and ours, matter.

Hildegard in Historical Context: "God's Mouthpiece" in a Time of Turmoil

Born in the summer of 1098 in Bermersheim, Germany, twelve miles from the city of Mainz, Hildegard was thrust upon the stage of life in an era on the cusp, the close of one century and the dawning of the next. The period immediately preceding Hildegard, the Dark Ages, was a time when the supernatural and natural worlds were perceived as intertwined. The dawning of the Middle Ages, however, inaugurated a shift away from finding the holy in the midst of the natural world. At the same time, there existed a growing distance between clergy and laity in a Christianized Europe. The roles of wise women, midwives, healers, and counselors fell under new suspicions. (By 1233, fifty-four years after Hildegard's death, Pope Gregory IX established the Inquisition to root out witches, heretics, and other agents of Satan, who were believed to be spreading throughout Europe to destroy the clerical and political status quo.) The practice of seeing the divine in all things was eroding. The distrust of women and of nature was intimately connected. The development of sacramental theology and practice, especially the sacrament of penance, created a chasm between the daily life of an ordinary person and the extraordinary functioning of the ordained clergy, who alone dispensed the necessary graces for salvation.

Interestingly, there was concurrently a sense among mystics of the relationship between personal salvation and the interior life. That is, the notion of the soul and the inner self, as distinct from the outer world and the church, was being discovered as a realm of divine activity. Hildegard was born into this time of paradox, an epoch of spiritual fervor, extraordinary expansion of monastic life, and the simultaneous clericalization of the church. Conflicts over the centralization of papal power, the development of canon law, the modeling of church structure and authority on the feudal system, the institutionalization of the discipline of celibacy for clergy, and the growing corruption of a church bent on the Crusades led "poor and frail" women, like Hildegard, to challenge the learned masculine clergy to reform. Hildegard denounced her own period of history as an "effeminate age" in which men had grown lax and weak, and because of this women were called to prophesy. God would confound "them" by making women "virile" (Newman 1987, pp. 238–40). Hildegard said, "For when learned and powerful men are sunk into feminine levity, then men are scandalized by the preaching of women" (McNamara 1996, p. 350).

Hildegard was shaped in a historical, cultural, philosophical, and religious tradition that took for granted the inherent inferiority of the female. Hildegard accepted the natural and hierarchical ordering of creation. Within the social and religious structures of her time, everyone knew his or her place within the natural order as preordained by God *Himself*. Inherent female weakness required inherent masculine strength to maintain God's given order. While Hildegard equated the feminine with frailty, she was required to argue that it was God who chose the weak to shame the strong. In this regard, Hildegard's keen sense of feminine and masculine uniqueness foreshadowed Jung's notion of the *anima* and *animus* operative in each human personality. She had no recourse other than to invert gender roles, shown strikingly in some of her visual illuminations, so that women were seen as virile, strong, and virtuous, a prophetic counterpoint to the lax, corrupt, and "womanish" male leaders of her time. In using "womanish," Hildegard did not mean that the manliness was not evident in terms of bloodshed and war, but that men were womanish precisely because the justice of God had become weak in men's hands.

Hildegard's reference to herself as God's "mouthpiece" and "little trumpet" was all the more provocative because of her activity in the context of the Gregorian reforms unfolding during the eleventh and twelfth centuries. Hildegard was coming of age and finding her voice in an era when a pejorative depiction of women as seducers and temptresses abounded in the struggle to impose permanent celibacy on clergy. Her life bore alternative witness in the midst of the prevalent misogyny of the time.

Hildegard's age saw intense conflict between the empire and the papacy. The church was tied to the feudal system in which prelates received land and titles from secular leaders to whom they then owed allegiance. Bishops were clerics *and* soldiers. Emperors and popes had armies that fought one another over territorial ambitions. The twelfth century experienced the rise and fall of nearly a dozen antipopes. Kings and emperors made futile attempts to regain control of the papacy. The spread of heretical groups threatening to splinter the faithful coincided with a robust economy and the development of urban life. The sanctuaries and scriptoriums of monasteries were increasingly indebted to the endowments of the wealthy seeking spiritual benefits in return for financial support. Simony, the purchase of such favors as well as ecclesiastical offices, was rampant. The Crusades raged.

Hildegard preached about the consequences for such a church riddled with confusion and corruption, unwittingly prophesying the Protestant Reformation of the sixteenth century. She was a religious woman compelled by God to speak out about the negligence that riddled the pastoral care of the people of Christ's church and indeed, in her words, "the web of all creation." She chided kings and bishops: "The masters and the prelates sleep without troubling themselves any more about justice . . . those who let themselves go with woman's weakness will soon be punished for it" (Pernoud 1998, p. 13). In a letter to Pope Anastasias IV she wrote, "Wake up from the slumber of tolerance and fatigue in discernment" (Craine 1997, p. 29). She scolded clerics for their folly and material ambition, saying, "They wish to have glory without merit and merit without work" (McNamara 1996, p. 350).

As Hildegard connected her theology with her politics, she also made connections between how humans interact with one another and with the actual world around them. As she cautioned leaders about their lax approach to the affairs of the world and church, she also reproached them regarding their relation to the natural world. She said, "Human beings cannot live without the rest of nature, so they must care for all natural things" (Van de Weyer 1997, p. 42), and "If human beings abuse their position of power over the rest of God's creation, then God will allow other creatures to rise up and punish them. Do not regard other creatures as existing merely to serve your bodily needs. By cherishing them as God requires, your soul will benefit . . . . All nature is at the disposal of humankind. We are to work with it. Without it we cannot survive (ibid., p. 41). In this regard, Hildegard reveals the interconnectedness of her vision of life. All facets of life are interdependent. Here again she foreshadows future events—the rise in the twentieth century of ecological crises, environmental concerns, and animal rights.

It is significant that Hildegard began to write a decade after the Council of Clermont of 1130 forbade those in vowed religious orders to be active, which would include practicing medicine. It was common for monasteries to have infirmaries that reached beyond their own members to care for the sick and dying in the communities that surrounded their enclosed life. Only two medical books were written in the West in the twelfth century, both attributed to Hildegard: *Physica (Natural History or the Book of Simple Medicine)* and *Cause et cure (Causes and Cures)*. These particular writings have resulted in her being called the first woman doctor and first woman scientist (Maddocks 2001, p. 147). The decision to wrest healing practices away from monks and nuns contributed to the secularization of medicine and the split between science and natural healing, between the cure of the body and the care of the soul. This split would not be finalized until the Inquisition inaugurated by Pope Gregory IX in 1233—fifty-four years after Hildegard's death. Not surprisingly, Hildegard and her nuns did not accept these impending divisions, and her legacy reveals, again foreshadows, a commitment to holism, the unity of body/mind/spirit so prevalent in the contemporary practice of spirituality and healing in medicine today.

Hildegard wrote prolifically between the ages of forty-two and eighty-one. In addition to her two major works on medicine and natural science, Hildegard completed a trilogy of theological works: the multimedia illuminated manuscript for which she is most famous, *Scivias* (abbreviated from the Latin for *Know the Ways of the Lord*), the *Book of Life's Merits* (also translated as the *Book of the Rewards of Life*), and the *Book of Divine Works*. She composed seventy-seven liturgical songs and recorded them in the *Symphonia: The Symphony of the Harmony of Celestial Revelations*. She wrote commentaries on the Rule of St. Benedict and the Creed. She was the biographer for the life of St. Disibod and St. Rupert, Celtic missionaries to the Rhineland. Fifty of her homilies and more than three hundred letters from her active correspondence remain (see *The Letters of Hildegard of Bingen*, 1994, 1998, and 2004). Her correspondents included Henry II of England, Eleanor of Aquitane, Bernard of Clairvaux, Popes Eugenius III, Anatasius IV, Adrian IV, and Alexander III; Emperors Konrad III and Frederick Barbarossa, and the Archbishops of Mainz, Trier, and Saltzburg. Her letters also include exchanges with abbots and abbesses, other women mystics and nuns, and lay people seeking her counsel (Lerner 1993, p. 55).

Hildegard's courage and creativity are the stuff of legend and legacy. Historian Gerda Lerner says "the life of Hildegard of Bingen exemplifies the breakthrough of a female genius who managed to create an entirely new role for herself and other women without ostensibly violating the patriarchal confines within which she functioned" (1997, p. 52). "If Hildegard had been a male theologian," speculates Barbara Newman, "her *Scivias* would undoubtedly have been considered one of the most important early medieval summas" (quoted in *Scivias* 1990, p. 23). Medical historian Heinrich Schipperges calls Hildegard a "unique phenomenon in Western intellectual history" (1997, p. 28), and Matthew Fox, in his foreword to the *Book of Divine Works*, says "she contributed substantially to the awakening to a living cosmology and to the influx of women's experience into the mystical literature of the West" (1987, p. xi). Hildegard has been referred to as a proto Protestant because of her caustic attack on clerical abuses. She called for no less than a reformation and prophesied that if a "virile age" did not return, there would be "a confiscation of ecclesiastical wealth by princes and the dissolution of monasteries." Such would indeed come to pass. Hildegard of Bingen lived and thrived, albeit painfully, in a time of political and religious tumult not so different from our own. "Her sheer force of will," Newman says, "combined with a dazzling array of spiritual and intellectual gifts, a courage hardened by decades of struggle, and a prophetic persona, which she displayed in season and out, made her a formidable opponent; and she did not take defeat easily" (*Scivias* 1990, p. 15).

A Formidable, Fragile Female

With the broad strokes of Hildegard's historical context in place and an initial sense of her formidable presence and productivity, let us glance at some of the shaping events in Hildegard's life journey. Understanding the influences that gave rise to a woman who by all logic ought not to have existed provides a lens through which to see more clearly the reasons behind her reemergence today, a reemergence that represents both a secularization and internationalization of Hildegard studies achieved in less than two decades (see Sabina Flanagan's preface in McInerney 1998, p. xiii).

Early Years: The Formation of a Spiritual Architect

Following the custom of noble families, Hildegard's parents tithed their tenth child, Hildegard, as a tribute to the Lord when she was eight years old. While there is evidence that Hildegard agreed to this dedication of her young life, in the *Scivias* (II, V) she writes a strong objection to the practice of dedicating children to monasteries without their consent, "thereby delivering him [her] up by the worst of deceptions." Her parents entrusted her to the care of twenty-year-old Jutta von Spanheim, a pious noblewoman. Rather than immediately entering the anchorage (from the Greek, "to withdraw") at the renovated Benedictine monastery on Mt. Disibodenberg, as previously thought, it now seems more likely that Hildegard, along with one or two other girls, remained at Spanheim under Jutta's tutelage for a few years. The anonymous *Life of Jutta* indicates that in 1112, Jutta, Hildegard, and possibility one other young woman took residence as recluses in a small convent attached to the newly rebuilt monastery of Disibodenberg (see Silvas 1998). This was a widespread practice in the twelfth century. Hildegard professed her religious vows as a Benedictine nun at the age of fifteen or sixteen.

During these formative years, Hildegard watched as the original seventh-century Disibodenberg site was reconstructed into a small twelfth-century medieval city that included the female anchorage, followed by a larger convent, a parish church, hospital, mill, gardens, refectory, monastery for the monks, vineyards, and a scriptorium. It is interesting to speculate that Hildegard's own desire to build an independent monastery, which she eventually did, found roots in a fertile mind fueled by observing the activity around her. It is as if the building going on around her imprinted her young imagination with the design of her own future as a spiritual architect.

Inseeing

Jutta was an able *magistra* (leader) for her small band of child learners and spiritual seekers. Unlike her female contemporaries, Hildegard would enjoy the benefit of an education steeped in the monastic way of life. An unusual child, Hildegard confided in Jutta: "When I was three years old, I saw an immense light that shook my soul; but, because of my youth, I could not externalize it" (Sur 1993, p. 26). This light within her soul she would eventually name the *umbra viventis lucis*: a spiritual inseeing and reflection of the Living Light, happening day or night, in full consciousness, and in multicolor brilliance accompanied by a "hearing in the soul":

> I do not hear [visions] with my outward ears, nor do I perceive them by the thoughts of my own heart or by any combination of my five senses. I hear them in my soul alone while my outward eyes are open. I have thus never fallen prey to ecstasy in the visions, but see them wide-awake, by day and by night. (Craine 1997, p. 36)

It has been said that Hildegard's visual illuminations, which form the core of the *Scivias,* are best described as "theology in pictures." Her inner picturing is not a prop but a visionary inspiration of complexities of thought; the painted picture is "an attempt to make accessible to the external eye what the inner eye has perceived" (Pacht 1984, p. 160). In the commentary on "The Secret of the Golden Flower," Jung underscores the genuineness of such visionary experience. "The phenomenon itself, the vision of light," Jung says, "is an experience common to many mystics, and one that is undoubtedly of the greatest significance . . . . Hildegard of Bingen . . . writes in much the same way about her central vision" (1957, par. 42). More will be said about Hildegard's visionary experience in chapter 3.

Hildegard confided only in Jutta and her priest-confidant Volmar, who later became her secretary and trusted friend, in sharing the experiences of her visionary life. Hildegard remained silent as to the theological content of her visions. This imposed silence and its consequent physical debilitation enfolded itself in Hildegard's daily existence for the first twenty years of her life at Disibodenberg. In 1136, Jutta died at the age of forty-four. At the time of Jutta's death the little band of women had grown to seven. Hildegard, then thirty-eight, was elected abbess of the convent of nuns, although technically, she never officially received the title of abbess. The informal status of the anchorage did not meet the requirements for the position of abbess, so while she was commonly referred to as an abbess, officially her title was prioress or *magistra* (teacher).

The Grace of Office

It is important to note that although Hildegard lived in near seclusion for the greater part of her life, she was nonetheless aware of the problems of her times. Abbesses, especially those of noble birth like Hildegard, were engaged in those aspects of the world related to feudal ties and obligations. Parents offered dowries that accompanied their daughters to the nunnery and in return for money received spiritual benefits. Such negotiations at that time were seen as neither essentially corrupt nor morally manipulative, but simply part and parcel of accepted ecclesiastical transactions that sustained religious life. Hildegard listened to the concerns of the laity as they sought counsel through the anchorage window (see plate 1, Cynthia Large's portrait of Hildegard with crowd assembled outside her window). She engaged in all the activities of the Disibodenberg monastic city steeped in *ora et labora*—the rhythm of prayer and work—still characteristic of the Benedictine way of life today.

As Hildegard shouldered the mantle of abbess, she entered a role that brought her a new scope of authority. To some extent, the role of the abbess during the early medieval period enlarged the playing field for female religious leaders. The function of the abbesses was particularly vexing to canonists and popes precisely because of the scope of their authority. It was not uncommon for the abbess to be the magistrate over dual monasteries of both monks and nuns. The abbatial authority of medieval nuns included the power to hold councils with other abbesses and to leave the enclosure in order to be in dialogue with other abbeys and affiliated convents. The abbess held spiritual power to bless, proclaim the gospel, instruct, lead Eucharistic processions, and hear the confessions of her nuns. Such powers held by women in Hildegard's time were forbidden a century later and never returned to the domain of female religious leadership again, even to the present day (Labarge 1986, pp. 33, 101). In 1298, Pope Boniface VIII issued an edict of enclosure for nuns with the elimination of almost all of the independent ecclesiastical and liturgical powers of the abbess.

Breaking Silence

At the age of forty-three, in her early years as abbess, Hildegard finally broke her silence on her inner visions and their content. She was "instructed" by the Living Light "to put her hand to writing" and "release the power and mystery of hidden and marvelous visions." At the end of Jung's life he was asked if civilization would survive, and he responded that it would if enough people took responsibility for the awakening of their own inner life. Hildegard is such a midlife model of taking seriously the claims of one's interior homework. Suffice it to say here that in her early forties Hildegard took the first step of the next thirty-eight years of writing and public speaking. Her breakthrough to voice was not without its seasons of self-doubt, which pushed her to seek the counsel of Bernard of Clairvaux (1090–1153), the most important Cistercian monk of his time. A strict order of monks following the Rule of St. Benedict, the Cistercian's way of life was one of silence, in a community devoted mainly to liturgy and prayer. They followed strict dietary rules and were known as pioneers in agriculture. Hildegard appealed to Bernard in a letter as to whether she ought to continue to reveal her visions or remain silent, even though containing her inner life brought on psychic and physically painful manifestations. She was forty-nine and Bernard nearly sixty at the time. In a return letter dated 1146–47, Bernard acknowledged her gift as a grace and encouraged her to continue (see *The Letters of Hildegard of Bingen,* vol. 1, p. 31). Hildegard was uplifted by Bernard's response; his affirmation provided her the impetus to engage the ecclesial system to help her bring her words and images to print and visual expression. Thus, Abbot Kuno of Disibodenberg approved the appointment of the monk Volmar as her secretary, an unusual occurrence in the power arrangements of her time. Usually the women were at the service of the men.

Hildegard's theological, political, and spiritual leadership, nourished through her correspondence with Bernard of Clairvaux, and her intellectual and affectionate relationship with Volmar provide a window into the unique ways that medieval religious women and men established trust, confidence, and mutuality in a time in which societal configurations appeared to work against such gender balance. These relationships and those with the nuns of her community, particularly the young nun Richardis, created a milieu in which Hildegard could sustain the activity of her inner life and bring her first major work, *Scivias,* to completion over a ten-year period, 1141–1152.

To have her work legitimated by the church, a commission was sent to Disibodenberg to examine the partially completed *Scivias.* When completed, the *Scivias* was an illuminated manuscript of twenty-six visions with theological commentary addressing an array of Christian doctrine including Divine Majesty, the Trinity, creation, the fall, Incarnation, sacraments, virtues, and the end of the world. The commission also examined Hildegard herself. The examiners took their findings to the Synod of Trier, 1147–48, convened by Pope Eugenius III. With the support of the respected Bernard of Clairvaux, portions of the *Scivias* were read aloud to the assembled bishops. Bernard urged the pope "not to allow such a brilliant light to be covered by silence but rather to confirm this charism through his authority" (Craine 1997, p. 26). Pope Eugenius III and the Synod Fathers of Trier gave Hildegard apostolic license to continue and "commanded" her to complete her "divinely inspired" work. Such ecclesiastical sanction freed Hildegard into an unprecedented future that would, however, be abundant with further struggles and new challenges.

Paralysis and Power

Hildegard began to gain wider public notoriety as more people, from kings and emperors to peasants possessed by demons, sought her help. Donations poured into Disibodenberg in support of the *prophetessa* of the Rhine. The number of nuns in her care had grown to eighteen and the small accommodations were inadequate. Hildegard experienced a vision in which she was called to leave Disibodenberg and establish her own independent monastery. When she shared this revelation with Abbot Kuno, he summarily dismissed the possibility of such an undertaking. A move from Disibodenberg would mean the loss of attention due to Hildegard's growing fame, cutting the monks off from connections with local nobility and the material gifts offered for spiritual benefits. Hildegard, in a pattern that marked her life, was stricken with a severe malady. Her health alternated between periods of physical vitality and physical debilitation. She was filled with energy in times when she was advancing her outer and inner work and suffered terribly depleting episodes when she was impeded in realizing what she believed to be God's will.

This physical marvel is not uncommon among the rare personality with such an acute state of consciousness as Hildegard. Jung referenced Hildegard in the development of his own thinking on this phenomenon, which will be explored in more detail in chapter 3. Barbara Newman documents the contention that Hildegard's paralyzingly painful suffering would be diagnosed today as migraines, and she credits Hildegard as the first to make illness a dominant theme for female saints (see Burnett and Dronke 1998, pp. 197–204).

Eventually the Abbot came to see with his own eyes that the paralysis that turned Hildegard's body stonelike was the result of his interference with God's will. He reluctantly conceded, offering his permission for her to proceed. In character, Hildegard emerged from her sickbed animated with the passion of a new foundation to be located on the Rupertsburg, a mountain near Bingen, a day's journey, some nineteen miles from Disibodenberg.

Following her move to Rupertsburg in 1150, an exceptional action by one who described herself as "timid and lacking boldness," Hildegard made arrangements to acquire complete canonical and legal separation from the monks at Disibodenberg. She wanted to choose the monks who would provide spiritual care to the nuns at Rupertsburg, keep the dowries from the women's families who joined the congregation, call the free election of superiors, hold the deed to the property, and be accountable solely to the Archbishop of Mainz. Hildegard insisted this secret arrangement be put in writing, and she received it from the Archbishop of Mainz in 1158. She went even further in seeking political protection along with legal and canonical independence. In 1163, Frederick Barbarossa, king and emperor of Germany, issued an edict of imperial protection in perpetuity for Hildegard's Rupertsburg monastery (see John Van Engen in Newman 1998, pp. 39–40, and Dronke 1984, p. 153).

This is a striking example of Hildegard's celebrity reaching to the highest levels of authority and involving even those whom she previously chastised. Hildegard had once rebuked Emperor Frederick Barbarossa, going so far as to call him "insane," when he attempted to name, on two occasions, antipopes in the ongoing warfare over the papacy. She brazenly wrote, "O king, it is of utmost necessity that you take care of how you act. In the mysterious vision, I see you are acting like a child. You live an insane, absurd life before God. There is still time" (Craine 1997, p. 29). It seems that the plucky twelfth-century Abbess Hildegard was indeed a nun in politics—an anathema in twenty-first-century Catholicism.

The twenty nuns who went with Hildegard to begin the foundation at Rupertsburg resisted the harsh life they encountered in carving the monastery from the mountain and erecting it from the ground up. The imprint of Disibodenberg's construction embedded in Hildegard's memory now took wing. She supervised the construction of a twelfth-century monastery with indoor plumbing, a complete sewage system, and a hospice for the sick and dying. By the time the Rupertsburg monastery was finished, it stood out in grand relief on the hillside overlooking the confluence of the Nahe and Rhine Rivers. The community grew from twenty to fifty nuns. Rupertsburg remained an active monastery until the Swedes destroyed it in 1632 during the Thirty Years War. Only a small underground cavern in the deep foundation of the original site remains today.

A Woman of the Word

Amazingly, while Hildegard was overseeing a new foundation and seeking to establish her autonomy as an abbess, she completed the *Scivias* and the composition of *Physica*, also called *Natural History* or the *Book of Simple Medicine*. This work included a catalogue of plant life, precious stones, metals, fish and animals, as well as herbal and holistic healthcare remedies. She followed this with *Causes and Cures* (in Latin, *Cause et cure*), a medical text dealing with more than two hundred diseases and remedies for these illnesses. Included was a specific explanation about the physiology of sexual intercourse, conception, and childbirth, written from a female perspective. We find in her a mysteriously accurate understanding of the dynamics of sexual love and her original articulation of sexual complementarity.

In 1158, at age sixty, Hildegard undertook the first of four preaching tours, again quite extraordinary behavior for a medieval religious woman since only the ordained were permitted to preach by canon law. Of Hildegard's foray into preaching, McInerney notes, "A woman speaking in public at all was so remarkable that nothing she actually said could have seemed more astonishing than the simple fact of her speaking" (1998, p. xviii). She preached in cathedrals and town squares, to clergy and lay folk alike against the dualist threat of the Cathars, literally meaning the "pure ones." Catharism was a religious movement that broke away from the Church and was condemned as heretical. Maddocks characterizes the Cathars as follows:

They regarded the Catholic Church and the state as equally satanic, being part of the material world and thus evil. In addition to rejecting belief in hell, the resurrection, purgatory, meat, milk and eggs, they also denounced marriage, forbade sexual intercourse and held that suicide was both lawful and commendable. These extreme views, for all their undeniable purity, left few options for the survival of the human race. (2001, p. 217)

Since Hildegard's theology was holistic, seeing creation as good and lush with revelations of the Divine and human beings as bearing divine majesty, she railed against the Cathars as vigorously as she scolded clergy. Hildegard blamed the laxity of the clergy, their involvement in simony, military and political intrigues, and failure to preach the authentic gospel as the root cause of the rise of the Cathar heresy (Newman 1998, pp. 11, 20, 88).

No doubt prompted by the heresy she saw gaining ground as she traveled, Hildegard began the *Book of Life's Merits* (*Liber Vitae Meritorum*) at the close of her first preaching tour in 1158. Five years later, and in poor health, she completed this work, which presents six visions, all variations on the vision of the cosmic human being superimposed on the world. The text presents an animated symbolic conversation between thirty-five virtues and their attendant vices. Bruce Hozeski, founder of the International Society of Hildegard von Bingen Studies, says this book is one of the subtlest, most psychologically fascinating, and most intense works ever written on the relationship of the various sins to their corresponding virtues. Hozeski, in his foreword, suggests that while *Scivias* might be considered a handbook of belief, the *Book of Life's Merits* is a handbook of life (1997, p. xvii).

Also in 1163, Hildegard began the last of her visionary theological trilogy and most mature work, the *Book of Divine Works* (*De operatione Dei)*, which she completed in 1173–74. This book explores her cosmology in which she discloses the interdependency of humanity and creation as related to God and each other. She developed an eco-theological worldview in which "the microcosm reveals the macrocosm, and all of history was seen as salvation history" (Craine 1997, p. 29)

It is in the *Book of Divine Works* that Hildegard becomes the first to see woman as a symbol of normative humanity: "Man signifies the divinity of the son of God and woman his humanity" (Newman 1987, p. 93). In an innovative shift in theological anthropology, woman is the representative human being. Chapter 5 delves more deeply into Hildegard's vision of the sacredness of the female body in creating the body and blood of God's Incarnation—Jesus—through the woman Mary, the role of the feminine principle in the Trinity, the organic wholesome complementarity between man and woman—all themes, as well, in Jungian depth psychology.

In the midst of her preaching tours, managing the affairs of Rupertsburg, tending to the pastoral care of her nuns and those seeking her counsel, writing the *Book of Divine Works*, and maintaining an active correspondence regarding tumultuous secular and religious events, Hildegard, at age sixty-seven, fifteen years after founding Rupertsburg, decided to found another congregation at Eibingen in 1165. With thirty nuns, Hildegard set off down the east bank of the Rhine and established a new and final foundation on a site overlooking Rudesheim and across the river from Bingen. Hildegard continued to live at Rupertsburg but traveled twice weekly to Eibingen until her death.

Accomplishing Death

At this point, one would think that Hildegard's renown would have spared any further encumbrances on an elderly nun of such stature. Yet, even in the end time of life, she faced unexpected challenges. In this regard, Hildegard is a model of the conviction that old age does not exempt one from the unexpected happenings that require us, even in our final years, to make decisions that affect our well being and that of others. At eighty-one, Hildegard faced a final challenge. In this regard, Hildegard modeled what Jung, who died at eighty-six, meant when he said we needed to accomplish our death.

An excommunicated and seriously ill nobleman sought refuge at Rupertsburg. During his final days he received the sacraments and was reconciled with the church under Hildegard's supervision. He died and was buried in the consecrated ground of the monastery.

The authorities at Mainz heard about it and questioned the legitimacy of burying an excommunicant. They demanded that his body be exhumed and removed from the sacred ground. Hildegard refused the order with a clear announcement that the nobleman had died reconciled with God and the church. She and her nuns concealed the location of the burial site from the authorities. One has an image of an eighty-one-year-old nun dashing about a cemetery cleverly masking the site of the grave. One account suggests Hildegard and her nuns moved the body a few times to prevent it being detected. For this offense, she and her nuns were issued an interdict denying them the benefit of Mass and the Eucharist, as well as requiring the cessation of all sung prayer. The monastery went silent. A silent monastery, meaning one without sung prayer, was and is an oxymoron. The elderly abbess stood her ground even while publicly shamed.

Characteristically, she based her defiance of the order on her experience of the Living Light, which she considered to have greater authority than the earthly command given to her. She says, "I saw in my soul that, if we followed their command and exposed the corpse, such an expulsion would threaten our home with great danger . . . so we did not expose him" (for details, see Lerner 1993, p. 56; Dronke 1984, pp. 196–97; Newman 1998, p. 27; and *The Letters of Hildegard of Bingen*, vol. 1, pp. 76–83).

Unable to sing and to relish the "joy" of the Eucharist, the interdict placed another heavy burden on the aged Hildegard. Eventually the Archbishop of Mainz became convinced of the man's spiritual restoration and lifted the interdict. Hildegard died six months later on September 17, 1179, at the age of eighty-one.

Canonization processes began a mere forty-eight years after her death, but Hildegard was never formally canonized. On September 17, 1940—without ceremony—her name was added to the feast day calendar in Germany. In 1979, during the eight hundredth anniversary of her death, the German bishops petitioned Rome to have Hildegard of Bingen declared a Doctor of the Church and thus ranked with Teresa of Avila and Catherine of Siena, the only other two female Doctors of the Church. In 1997, Pope John Paul II declared a third female Doctor of the Church, not Hildegard, but

Therese of Lisieux, and only one hundred years following Therese's death at age twenty-four. Hildegard was once again overlooked, but it did not stifle her forceful and near-global reemergence into contemporary consciousness.

Application

Which episode in Hildegard's life most intrigued you?

Was there anything in her biographical sketch that captured your attention relative to your own life journey?

In what ways do you identify with her?

In what ways does she challenge you?

Hildegard suffered physically and emotionally when she suppressed her truth. When she decided in her forties to release her inner light a flood of insight, creativity, and energy poured forth. Did her struggle for authenticity and expression touch any desires within you at this time of your life?

CHAPTER 2

Hildegard's Reemergence into Contemporary Consciousness

Hildegard comes to us today because we need her.

—Nancy Fierro, CSJ, *Hildegard of Bingen and Her*
Vision of the Feminine

Why is it that we are especially interested
in psychology just now? The answer is
that everyone is in desperate need of it.

—C. G. Jung, *The Symbolic Life*

Hildegard seems to have lifted herself from obscurity and walked into the center of contemporary conversation more than eight hundred years after her death. The breadth of her contributions in music, theology, ecology, cosmology, science, poetry, mysticism, ethics, and the healing arts have found renewed favor in the late twentieth and early twenty-first centuries. From popular books such as Fournier-Rosset's *From Saint Hildegard's Kitchen: Foods of Health, Foods of Joy* to the scholarly *Voice of the Living Light: Hildegard of Bingen and Her World,* edited by Barbara Newman, or the meticulously researched *Hildegard of Bingen: The Woman of Her Age* by Fiona Maddocks; from the growing discography of Hildegard's original music to the electronic rendition of her morality play, *Ordo Virtutum (Play of theVirtues),* performed by the NewYork Hildegurls or the addition of her chant to chic background music; from Joan

Ohanneson's novel *Scarlet Music: Hildegard of Bingen* to "a future major motion picture . . . a romantic tale of love, power, and victory . . . *Breath of God: The* True *Story of Hildegard von Bingen,*" we seem to find her everywhere. Why? I'd like to suggest seven reasons for her reemergence into contemporary consciousness.

An Archeological Endeavor

Recovering models of strong and creative women was an archaeological endeavor for feminists in the last half of the twentieth century. The reappearance in the modern era of Hildegard of Bingen is credited to the search to locate the historical roots and routes of women's contribution to Western civilization. It is no surprise that in 1979, the eight hundredth anniversary year of her death, Hildegard found a place setting at controversial artist Judy Chicago's monumental landmark piece *The Dinner Party*, where Hildegard sits with thirty-nine other women at a triangular table measuring forty-eight feet on each side (see plates 2 and 3). *The Dinner Party* comprises a massive ceremonial banquet with each place setting consisting of embroidered runners, gold chalices and utensils, and painted porcelain plates. Beneath the table, the ceramic lusterware tiles covering the heritage floor are inscribed with the names of nine hundred and ninety-nine other outstanding women, including Jutta, contextualizing the women represented around the table in a grand historical display of female achievement. In 1979, although she had a place at Judy Chicago's *Dinner Party*, most viewers in North America knew little, if anything, about Hildegard.

Because we are denied knowledge of our history,
we are deprived of standing upon each other's shoulders
and building upon each other's hard-earned accomplishments.
Instead we are condemned to repeat what others have done before us
and thus we continually reinvent the wheel.
The goal of *The Dinner Party* is to break this cycle.

—Judy Chicago

It is clear that her belated emergence as a major representative of the twelfth century is due to two factors: the inspired diligence of the Benedictine communities in preserving and promoting Hildegard's legacy century after century, and the dogged quest in the late twentieth century to write women back into history. As historian Gerda Lerner so eloquently states, Hildegard "overcame the biggest obstacle all thinking women face and still face, the overwhelming burden of proving their right and their ability to think at all in opposition to tradition gender roles they were expected to fill" (1993, p. 57). The British novelist, historian, and literary critic Marina Warner chose Hildegard's *Scivias* as her "book of the millennium." Hildegard of Bingen is one story in the large sweep of historical imagination denied women for centuries. Hildegard of Bingen was one of the most prolific female authors of the medieval era. By bringing her past into our present, we connect with our roots and, in turn, give wings to a new future. We refuse to forget her ever again. Our refusal to forget her shapes a future for generations to come that will not have to rediscover her all over again.

The Mind/Body/Soul Connections

While the dominant medical system still suffers from a vision constructed on an illness model where various diagnosable physical or psychiatric symptoms are treated, often unrelated to the whole of the person's actual life, there is hope. Many North American health care facilities, including Loyola University Medical Center (Maywood, Illinois), announce that their mission is to "treat the whole person . . . the human spirit too." Conventional medicine is more open to exploring the psychospiritual origins of illness. The early years of the twenty-first century reveal rapid advancements in science in developing new approaches to understanding how mind, body, and emotions interact. Physicians at Harvard University's Mind/Body Medical Institute are working to establish mind/body science as an accepted part of mainstream academic medicine. Organizations such as the John Templeton Foundation seek to promote a deeper understanding of the influence of spirituality on human health. The Templeton Foundation, for example, supports collaboration and clinical research into the relationship between spirituality and health, and by documenting the positive medical aspects of spiritual practice, the Foundation is committed to contributing to the reintegration of faith into modern life. The popularity of the bimonthly magazine *Spirituality and Health: The Soul/Body Connection*, which reaches 200,000 readers six times a year, is further evidence of these interests among North Americans.

A renewed interest in retrieving the monastic traditions of cure of the body and care of the soul, herbal arts, and alternative therapies that honor the mind/soul/body connection have proliferated and are achieving validation within the mainstream medical community. Those involved in new medicine, art therapy, music therapy, bodywork therapy, homeopathic medicine, and other methods of advancing human flourishing and well-being find a visionary companion in the lifework of twelfth-century Hildegard. Two such native companions of Hildegard's natural and spiritual remedies are the coauthors of *Hildegard of Bingen's Medicine* (Strehlow and Hertzka 1988), which has sold over 30,000 copies. Gottfried Hertzka, M.D., and Wighard Strehlow founded the Hildegard Center in southern Germany. Europe has long been a fertile site for practicing Hildegard's medical theories. Hertzka, now retired, is credited with reviving modern interest in Hildegard's medicine and worked clinically with Hildegard's medicinal theories for more than thirty years. Strehlow, the current director of the Hildegard Center, is a noted scholar of Hildegard of Bingen who promotes her nutrition methods, medical treatments, and body/soul connection worldwide.

Their work is aimed at the restoration of more organic models of health care that take seriously herbal medicine and premodern natural healing traditions. Their clinic and spa, named after Hildegard, is a contemporary witness to the integration of natural medicine with spirituality, the connections between physiological disharmony—illness of the body—and the underlying disharmonies of the soul. In *Hildegard of Bingen's Spiritual Remedies* (2002), Strehlow postulates that 80 percent of the population of the Western world suffers and dies from illnesses, such as heart disease, stroke, and some cancers, that are autoaggressive. In short, he is saying that we are killing ourselves by failing to pay attention to the underlying spiritual malady, the soul sickness, which masks itself in physiological symptoms. These diseases remain deadly precisely because physicians often treat them on the physical level alone through surgeries, chemotherapies, and medications. Strehlow says, "Today we know through countless studies what Hildegard revealed eight hundred years ago: that lifestyle affects the so-called autonomic nervous system. Negative feelings such as hate, anger, and fear as well as positive emotions like love, compassion, and joy exert a strong influence on the autonomic nervous system, causing either health or disease" (2002, p. 56). For Hildegard, disease was not actually pathogenic, but the consequence of deficiencies and neglect.

For Hildegard, true healing can never be achieved from an outer source alone. Healing is a multidimensional process. Bodily health requires an inner consciousness. Hildegard's insights on sickness and methods of healing—arising from her own experience of debilitating illnesses—include awareness that human faculties and potentialities not expressed become symptoms in search of healing. When we bury human potential we create pathology. Hers is a biological spirituality in which each human cell contained the divine spark, whose aim was to bring the person to a fullness of life. Clearly, Hildegard's ideas will participate in the evolution of new medicine in the third millennium.

The Return of Virtues

Virtue is like a warm garment in a cold world.
It is the source of charm in a harsh world.

—Hildegard, *Scivias* 1.1.4

Recently there has been a resurgence of interest in virtues and the formation of the human character. A number of contemporary cultural critics from diverse backgrounds are speaking and writing about the need for a reexamination of ways to assist the young in developing character by exploring the role of virtues in the shaping of good, humane citizens. Interest in empirical studies on the importance of emotional and spiritual intelligence as indicators of the mature person is indicative of a substantive trend. In 2009, the University of Chicago launched the New Science of Virtues Project (www.scienceofvirtues.org), providing research grants for scholars and scientists from around the world to explore ways that the humanities and the sciences cooperate in developing richer understandings of the roles virtues play in modern societies. Hildegard most surely would have applied! Her work in the area of virtues corresponds to the questions guiding this twenty-first-century venture: How are the virtues understood? Why is virtue important? How do we know a virtue when we see one? What about virtue is fundamental or foundational to human beings and to a decent human society? What are the social, psychological, and biological impacts of virtues? How are virtues exemplified in the lives of individuals and in collectivities?

Hildegard authored the first known liturgical morality play in the West, *Ordo Virtutum* or *Play of the Virtues*. Virtues, for Hildegard, are not simply moral habits but therapeutic forces within the human character and within the cosmos itself. Virtues were naturally implanted means of self-realization. Striving for union with the Transcendent, for Hildegard, is an intrinsic impulse of human life and growth. Therefore, virtues have a physiological basis and therapeutic function, as well as illustrating a vision of the optimal person-in-society, especially important for a culture in crisis such as Hildegard's.

Hildegard places her play at the very end of the *Scivias*. Quite likely Hildegard's nuns performed this work at the consecration of the Rupertsburg monastery. It is possible that the monk Volmar, Hildegard's secretary, played the lone male role. The characters are all personifications. Interestingly, the heroine is named Anima, who along with her companion Souls, confronts the villain, Diabolus, in an animated sung drama with a chorus of sixteen virtues. Anima, the Souls, and all the virtues are feminine. The entire play is sung except when the devil (the ultimate vice) appears on stage. He alone, the only male personification, speaks his utterances. Hildegard's richly textured imagery dramatizes the conflict of Anima—feminine soul—struggling for the power to engage the forces of evil, symbolized by the devil. The virtues prevail in the end, and a limp Diabolus is carried off stage. The play is enjoying popularity on college campuses and is part of the revival of interest in the reclamation of the virtuous life.

While the *Scivias* pursued the exploration of the dynamic of the triumph of virtue over vice in human life, Hildegard's *Book of Life's Merits* (*Liber Vitae Meritorum*) continues to probe the inner struggle of human beings striving for inner and outer harmony—intrapsychically, interpersonally, and socially. Hildegard develops this virtue-vice debate with great insight into the intricacies of the human psyche. The *Book of Life's Merits* reveals the interplay of vices and virtues as conflicts within the soul. She explores thirty-five creative spiritual forces and thirty-five destructive spiritual forces (see the table on p. 37). The goal is to bring these forces into balance. We learn to hold the opposites in healthy harmony. Hildegard's pattern of seeing the opposites operative in each human personality parallels Jung and fits the current conversation on the recovery of virtue, as well as revealing Hildegard's prescient awareness of the reality of the complex mystery of the human psyche, a basis of the modern science of psychology.

Hildegard and Depth Psychology

The interests of those pursuing deeper understanding of the human psyche inevitably draw them to rediscover Hildegard in their search for multidimensional and multidisciplinary approaches to probing the potentials of the human personality. This rediscovery suggests that Hildegard could easily have been the poster woman for the invention of modern depth psychology and a good friend of Carl Gustav Jung. Some speculate that Hildegard foreshadowed depth psychology, which, from a Jungian perspective, takes seriously the rich world of the unconscious and is convinced that spirituality is essential to personal and collective human wholeness. This book brings into focus Jung's acknowledgment of the importance of Hildegard by exploring the context and meaning of Jung's seven references to Hildegard in his *Collected Works*. Many today across cultural and religious traditions are asking if it is possible for

LIBER VITAE MERITORUM
(THE BOOK OF VIRTUES AND VICES)

VICES	VIRTUES
1. *Amor saeculi* (material love)	*Amor caelestis* (heavenly love)
2. *Petulantia* (petulance)	*Disciplina* (discipline)
3. *Joculatrix* (love of entertainment)	*Verecundia* (love of simplicity)
4. *Obduratio* (hard-heartedness)	*Misericordia* (compassion)
5. *Ignavia* (cowardice, resignation)	*Divina victoria* (God's victory)
6. *Ira* (anger, criminality)	*Patientia* (tranquillity)
7. *Inepta laetitia* (inappropriate mirth)	*Gemitus ad Deum* (yearning for God)
8. *Ingluvies ventri* (gluttony)	*Abstinentia* (abstinence)
9. *Acerbitas* (bitterness of heart)	*Vera largitas* (generosity)
10. *Impietas* (wickedness, infamy)	*Pietas* (devotion)
11. *Fallacitas* (lying)	*Veritas* (truth)
12. *Contentio* (contention)	*Pax* (peace)
13. *Infelicitas* (unhappiness)	*Beatitudo* (blessedness)
14. *Immoderatio* (immoderation anarchy)	*Discretio* (discretion, moderation)
15. *Perditio animarum* (doom)	*Salvatio animarum* (salvation)
16. *Superbia* (arrogance)	*Humilitas* (humility)
17. *Invidia* (envy)	*Charitas* (charity)
18. *Inanis gloria* (thirst for glory)	*Timor Domini* (reverence for God)
19. *Inobedientia* (disobedience)	*Obedientia* (obedience)
20. *Infidelitas* (lack of faith)	*Fides* (faith)
21. *Desperatio* (despair)	*Spes* (hope)
22. *Luxuria* (obscenity)	*Castitas* (chastity)
23. *Injustitia* (injustice)	*Justitia* (justice)
24. *Torpor* (lethargy)	*Fortitudo* (fortitude)
25. *Oblivio* (oblivion)	*Sanctitas* (holiness)
26. *Inconstantia* (instability)	*Constantia* (stability)
27. *Cura terrenorum* (concern for worldly goods)	*Caeleste desiderium* (heavenly desire)
28. *Obstinatio* (obstinacy)	*Compunctio cordis* (remorse, compunction)
29. *Cupiditas* (craving)	*Contemptus mundi* (letting go)
30. *Discordia* (discord)	*Concordia* (concord)
31. *Scurrilitas* (scurrility)	*Reverentia* (reverence)
32. *Vagatio* (vagabondage)	*Stabilitas* (stability)
33. *Maleficium* (occultism)	*Cultus Dei* (dedication to God)
34. *Avaritia* (avarice)	*Sufficientia* (satisfaction)
35. *Tristitia saeculi* (melancholy)	*Caeleste gaudium* (heavenly joy)

Source: Wighard Strehlow, *Hildegard of Bingen's Spiritual Remedies* (Rochester, Vt.: Healing Arts Press, 2002), p. 40.

people in the twenty-first century to have interior visions that are
not reduced to psychosis or chicanery. Hildegard's biography as
well as her creative productivity is in and of itself a definition of
what Jung meant by individuation: the lifelong process of human
development that leads to the conscious awareness of wholeness
(Stein 1998, p. 233).

Hildegard's unique approach to examining virtues/vices as
imprints or images within the soul resonates with Jung's notion of
archetypes. Archetypes are innate patterns of thought, imagination,
or behavior that are universal. For Hildegard, virtues were far more
than mere habits; they were innate forces within, very similar to
Jung's conviction that archetypes, because they are found in human
beings in all times and places, exist in the human psyche waiting to
be activated (Stein, 1998, p. 233). The antithetical pairs of virtues/
creative forces and vices/destructive forces are part of the existential
anxiety of human life and living from which no one escapes.

Hildegard's appreciation for the feminine in God, quaternity
in the Trinity, and her theory of sexual complementarity link her
to Jung's discovery of the inner world of dreams and symbols,
the breadth and scope of the interior life, and the reality of the
anima and *animus*, archetypal images of the eternal feminine and
the eternal masculine respectively. The *anima* is the feminine in
man's unconscious and the *animus* is the masculine in woman's
unconscious. It is interesting to note that Hildegard's understanding of sexual complementarity has less to do with the sexual
theology of St. Augustine and more to do with the ways in which
male and female partnership mutually work to enhance wholeness
in each other.

Finally, Hildegard's uncanny sense of the dark side of life
and her insistence that individuals must take responsibility for
destructiveness most strikingly links to the notion of the personal
and collective shadow in depth psychology. Hildegard's call for
conversion among the negligent and corrupt clergy of her time,
her awareness of the collective impact on nature of humankind's
irresponsibility toward the earth, and her keen sense of people's
difficulty in coming to terms with the painful aspects of their lives
and relationships poignantly reveals her understanding of the
personal and collective shadow—those rejected and unacceptable

parts of ourselves we repress in order to maintain the status quo of our personal and collective persona. When the shadow is denied, it inevitably projects itself destructively. It has been said that from a depth psychological point of view, when Jesus says to take up the cross and follow him, he meant to bear the burden of your own shadow. Hildegard once concluded a letter to an abbot whom she believed to be falling into complacency: "Wake up and bear your burdens!" (Schipperges 1997, 71). Thus, in a very real way Hildegard could have been a twentieth-century depth psychologist and Jung a twelfth-century mystic/scientist/artist.

Walk through the valley of humility and know peace.
Lose your titanic, hard-to-satisfy ego.
A greedy self-esteem is just a steep mountain you'll find
dangerous to climb. It's also tricky (if not impossible)
to come down from such heights, and anyhow
the summit is too small for community.
Focus on Love's splendid garden instead.
Gather the flowers of humility and simplicity of soul.
Study God's patience. Keep your eyes open.

—from a letter by Hildegard of Bingen, in
   Hildegard of Bingen: A Spiritual Reader

From the viewpoint of dogmatic Christianity, Jung was distinctly an "outsider." For all his world-wide fame, this verdict was forcibly borne in upon him by the reactions to his writings. This grieved him, and here and there in this book he expresses the disappointment of an investigator who felt that his religious ideas were not properly understood. More than once, he said grimly, "They would have burned me as a heretic in the Middle Ages!" Only since his death have theologians in increasing numbers begun to say that Jung was indubitably an outstanding figure in the religious history of our century.

—Aniela Jaffé, introduction to *Memories, Dreams, Reflections,* pp. x-xi

An Eco-Theologian

Hildegard, often referred to as a "creation" theologian, stresses God as Creator and the sacramentality of the created world in her writings. In Hildegard's ecological vision every aspect of the created universe is interconnected and interpenetrated: cosmos and creatures, nature and grace, body and spirit, elements of the earth and sacraments. She says, "Everything that is in the heavens, on the earth, and under the earth is penetrated with connectedness, penetrated with relatedness." Her positive regard for the created world as a mirror of God's own nature makes Hildegard a rich resource for modern Christian eco-theology and the development of ecofeminism. She opposes the notion that the earth as matter is evil and exists to be used and used up by those with power to dominate and disseminate the world's natural resources. Jung also supported the interconnectedness of all life. His perspectives on the interpenetration of psyche, nature, and spirit provide an empathic link to holism and foreshadowed the emergence of ecopsychology where interdependency reigns. The "near neighbor and far, this country and the one on the other side of the globe, rain forest and city, the spider and the human, matter and spirit, Earth and cosmos" are all connected (Ulanov 1999, p. 77). Hildegard's natural theology and mystical approaches to nature are yet more examples of her holistic spiritual vision that appeal to so many in the first decade of a new century.

The concept of *viriditas*, her most novel theological invention, at the heart of her ecological theology and spirituality, is explored in chapter 7. Simply expressed, *viriditas* is the principle of all life, of all reality, emblematic of growth and fertility in all aspects of nature. *Viriditas* is the greening power of all creation; it is the green life force of the world. Greening power exists in animals, fish, birds, plants, rocks, trees, and flowers (*Book of Divine Works*, IV, 11). The concept of *viriditas* is significant to Hildegard's color theology. It bore a natural resemblance to the verdant lushness of creation and is the color of the soul—the green life force of the body. "There is a power in eternity, Hildegard once said, and it is green" (Schipperges 1997, p. 67) The entire cosmos is God's dwelling place, and humans are created to use their gifts to maintain the balance needed for a healthy organism, themselves and the whole of the earth working in tandem. Her twelfth-century reflections expressed the reciprocal influence of the environment on humans and humans on the environment. The mishandling of the earth by humans throws the whole cosmos out of harmony. There is almost an eerie foreshadowing of the catastrophic outcomes should humanity continue to tamper with nature. "Winds will stink with putrefaction . . . air vomits forth dirt . . . pollution obscured with light . . . all the elements and all creatures cry aloud at the blaspheming of nature and at wretched humankind's devotion of so much of its short life to the rebellion against God . . . This is why nature complains so bitterly about humanity" (from the *Liber Vitae Meritorum*, translated in Schipperges 1997, p. 57). In 1930, Abbot Ildefons Herwegen noted that there was "no other medical person who came anywhere near to attaining her profound understanding of the invisible web of nature or her universal empathy with the elements of creation" (ibid., p. 63). She has been called an ecological prophet and this is yet another reason for her renaissance in our era of inconvenient truths, climatic changes, and ecological crises.

The Music of Her Visions

It is perhaps for her music that Hildegard is best known. Her compositions have actually enjoyed a celebrated place in the history of medieval music. This is an area of Hildegard's work that has attracted prolonged scholarly interest. It is only recently, however, that her music made the best-seller charts of the recording industry with new releases of her medieval chant. Fiona Maddocks says, "The surprise Hildegard breakthrough, as it might be called, came in 1983 when *A Feather on the Breadth of God*—the title borrowed from the *Scivias*—won a coveted *Gramophone* Award" (2001, p. 189).

In 1998, the nine hundredth anniversary of her birth, the vocal quartet Anonymous 4 released their Hildegard album, *11,000 Virgins: Chants for the Feast of St. Ursula* (one of Hildegard's original compositions). It sold 30,000 copies that year, and the recording was number five on *Billboard's* classical list. Contemporary groups such as Anonymous 4, Sequentia, Tapestry, and Gothic Voices are experiencing what Hildegard believed: music is the highest form of human activity, mirroring the sounds of the choirs of angels and the inner life of each soul, which itself is like a symphony. Hildegard's *Symphonia* best illustrates the contemporary magnet of her music. *The Symphony of the Harmony of Celestial Revelation* is Hildegard's masterpiece of lyric poetry set to music. The title is meant to convey not only the divine source of the songs but also that the singing and the receiving of the sounds convey the grace to experience the same inner intensity that illumined her. Appealing to the Prelates at Mainz to lift the silence imposed upon her monastery in 1178–79, Hildegard wrote, "Music stirs our hearts and engages our souls in ways we can't describe. When this happens, we are taken beyond our earthly banishment back to the divine melody Adam knew before . . . Remember that singing is our best hope to hear divine harmony again" (*Letters of Hildegard of Bingen*, vol. I, pp. 76–79; quoted from Butcher 2007, pp. 124–126).

Medical historian Heinrich Schipperges comments that in Hildegard humanity and the cosmos existed as if in musical concord—a symphony—bringing about a consonance in human souls. Music served not only as a guide to healthy living but functioned as a basis for an effective system of therapeutic healing (1997, p. 19). Music was a therapeutic agent directed to a person's inner life. "For every element has its own sound, a pristine sound in God's created order, and all the tones blend into one universal harmony" (ibid., p. 86). All the arts were divinely inspired. Music held a singular place in the medieval religion of healing, particularly ministering to the sick and dying. Benedictine monasticism placed care of the sick above all other monastic works; the hospices of medieval monasteries predated palliative care by eight hundred years.

The pioneering work in music-thanatology of internationally recognized harpist, educator, and clinician Therese Schroeder-Sheker, founder of the Chalice of Repose Project, is a stellar example of the contemporary application of music aligned with a Benedictine and Hildegardian vision.[1] Schroeder-Sheker says, "The practical spiritual inspiration for the work of music-thanatology is monastic medicine, with its astute twofold regime of 'care of the body, cure of the soul'" (2001, p. 24).

Music-thanatology is a contemplative practice with clinical applications; through decades of hard work, it has been fully accepted into the medical model as a palliative medical modality. It uses prescriptive music—music individualized to meet the needs of each patient—and is delivered live, at the bedside, with voice and harp. No recorded music is ever used, and no two deliveries of music would ever be the same, for the entire human being as well as the dynamism of their illness is taken into account. Prescriptive music reflects the patient's constitution, temperament, breathing patterns, pulse, temperature, and blood pressure and couples them to the details of the illness prognostications. The goal of music-thanatology is twofold, addressing both the physiological pain and the interior suffering of the person who is actively dying. Ultimately, the contemplative dimension of the work offers the suffering, both patient and loved ones, the attentive gift of a musical presence of being. This in turn protects and facilitates the possibility of depth, reverence, beauty, and intimacy, even in the hospital or intensive care unit where the medical terrain is highly technological. In that context, the music-thanatologist offers very practical, measurable relief from the emotional, physical, and spiritual pain that so often accompanies dying. Music-thanatology is an evidence-based practice but emphasizes the possibility of a blessed, peaceful, or conscious death and affirms the language of monastic medicine. In employing the word *transitus*, the deathbed journey is recognized as an essential part of a human continuum, replete with movement and transition. The dying one is literally crossing the threshold from one way of being to another. In the Christian world, the day of one's death has often been called the *dies natalis*, indicating birth into new life. But the moral foundation of medicine is the inestimable worth of every single person, and a large percentage of Americans are dying outside of the support of faith traditions. "Make no mistake," Schroeder-Sheker says:

> the people for whom we receive referrals come from every walk of life, every religious identity, and *no* religious identity, but they are human, they are suffering, they are our brothers and sisters. Some are alone and frightened, some are surrounded by loved ones. They are young and old, male and female, agnostic

and atheist, baptized and bar-mitzvahed. Those particulars gradually fall away as the most essential elements remain. All have heartbeat and breath, and need something vast or profound that chemo can't provide. Despite the brevity of the time together, the possibility of the genuine I-Thou encounter is powerful and palpable, and no one ever feels the need to name it. (personal communication, 2008)

Schroeder-Sheker works fully in the world, yet she is a lay Benedictine who has, since childhood, been deeply inspired by the vision of monasticism and by the women mystics. "Hildegard shouldered non-stop responsibilities," she said, "but she protected and cultivated her inner life, her spiritual life." As academic dean of the Chalice of Repose Project's School of Music-Thanatology and clinical supervisor to dozens of music-thanatology graduate students nationwide, Schroeder-Sheker lives what she calls an *interiorized monasticism*. It is precisely the contemplative dimension of that commitment that has allowed her to sustain a dual lifework in the care of the dying, concurrent to the world of classical music. "Without that, I couldn't work in the trenches, where we're needed," she says, "Working with the dying means you are always saying 'Yes!' to the Unknown." This contemplative dimension stands in marked contrast to the highly technological delivery of medicine embedded in hospital cultures everywhere. When asked about some of the Hildegard influences in her life, Therese Schroeder-Sheker was very specific:

It would be easy for others to imagine that it is her music alone, or her sapiential theology that inspires me, but I don't literalize her sequences and hymns or her medical treatises into music-thanatology practice *per se*. On the other hand, when you look more deeply, you'll find her signature, her "fingerprint," everywhere in our ranks, starting with the centrality of the harp.

There is no indication whatsoever that Hildegard or her sisters ever had a physical harp, yet it is the instrument that shows up the most frequently in her visions. At one point, she had a vision of Christ with three harps at his sacred heart. Why?

How? What does this mean? She doesn't literalize the harp into technique or repertoire; she takes it up as a perfect symbol for mystical teaching. Everything about strings anchored deep within a body, a sound box, and stretching vertically, seemingly beyond capacity, speaks to the necessity of groundedness in an active spirituality that is beautiful and attuned.

By extension, strings being tuned and retuned exteriorizes much about the inner life and the process of *metanoia,* that gradual stripping away of the unconscious, habituated, out-of-tune, off-the-mark ways of being/doing. *Metanoia* always results in the transformation of the whole person, including the flowering of new virtues, those forces that are lived out in life and community and benefit the whole world. In the metaphor of tuning, we find both spiritual and psychological indications. Everything about going flat or sharp, pushing and asserting, or the opposite, stepping back and withholding, is made audible, and provides a very strong picture of what it is we need to do and how we need to be to become proportional with others. And the many strings on the harp also represent the different kinds, sizes and shapes of people—everyone sounds differently, but unless we learn to sound together, we make chaos.

Hildegard's vision of the original Adamic voice, a paradisal voice, unsullied, is also something for contemplative musicianship to take seriously, and to pray about. This voice points to transparency whereas a contemporary music education in any of the performing arts inherently cultivates the opposite, a stage persona, or worse, a culturally conditioned voice. Like Hildegard, we work with all our singers to help them find and liberate something authentic.

Then we have Hildegard's vision of wholeness; her perception of the truly human as composed of body, soul and spirit; the interconnectedness of the worlds within Nature, linking mineral, plant, and animal kingdoms to both human and angelic, and finding all five realms within the human being. Her recognition of the human being as the microcosm of the larger cosmos and receptive to the elements, the stars, the luminaries changes the way she understands anatomy. She does not suffer from the mechanized picture of the human body that invaded thought with the Enlightenment. Likewise, her Böethian experience of music as an all pervading force streaming throughout the universe speaks to me deeply, and is not unrelated to the subtle things we experience at the deathbed. Hildegard's unashamed reception of a widened hearing (clairaudience) and seeing (clairvoyance) change the way we understand the senses, especially when people are extremely vulnerable. Her love of the entire natural world and all natural phenomena offers much to the serious clinician.

Her quite significant individuation process, so easily discerned by any Jungian today, is strong. She suffered, but eventually grew and had a formidable belief in herself. Even so, she was obedient! The transformative nature of her charism with the written and sung word is something I have always paid attention to, she used words to transform, not so much to inform, and that requires a different posture. We have (as a model) her willingness to create new forms—cultural and liturgical—when old forms no longer serve. We have (as a model) her ability to speak truthfully at great risk; her ability to sacrifice a great deal in order to remain integral in times of tremendous political pressure. She was able to be heard amongst the clamor or closure of a male monastic culture and a hierarchical church. She was complex enough to be able to withstand the tensions of opposites and face all the large and small failures and imperfections in the institutions of her church, and in her own community, in herself, and yet remain faithful.

I love her integration and synthesis of both analytical and analogical modes of being and you will find that synthesis everywhere in our music-thanatology curriculum. A person couldn't become a music-thanatologist without developing both capacities to a high degree—the practice brings music, spirituality and medicine together in a whole new trinity. The *creativity* of her Eucharistic devotion and sacramental life reminds me all the time that loving and honoring tradition does not mean *stasis*. We have her boldness and perseverance as transformative models. She didn't give up; she climbed the mountain.

As I say these things, all kinds of details from her life are racing through my mind. Many a time did I take strength from her unheard-of preaching tours, or counsel to kings and monarchs—she wasn't a priest! As I prepared to deliver medical grand rounds at some of the most distinguished medical schools and teaching hospitals in the country, I have remembered Hildegard. What harpist has ever taught physicians? What harpist has ever been invited to teach pain rounds at Memorial Sloan Kettering? Harvard Deaconess? Johns Hopkins? You simply respond when they call.

When she and her community suffered the interdict, loss of the sacraments, loss of music, being silenced, as a result of a truly Christian act of social justice, she gave us an amazing model of nonviolent resistance that predated Gandhi and King by centuries. I don't know any professional in academia, medicine, business or religion who isn't, at some time during the course of their career, faced with a profoundly conflicted situation that requires the willingness to give up security in order to preserve personal or professional integrity. It may not come to that, but sooner or later, if you are carrying serious responsibility, some situation will arise, and we have to decide if we stand for anything or just maintain the status quo. Many people won't risk at that level, but she did, and that is profoundly moving and modern to me. Medicine is big business, and hospice in America is largely co-opted by the business model, so it takes a lot of love, vision, acuity and moral imagination to remain faithful to a vision of holism and to sustain that for decades. The same is true for higher education, where students perceive themselves as consumers, or seek utilitarian degrees to become financially secure, rather than to become more fully human. Our abbess would have resisted the intellectual materialism or the fragmentation that is our cultural malaise today.

It has been a major effort in my life to develop not only a curriculum, but also sensitivity toward formation. Hildegard was profoundly practical, but her understanding of study was transformative. The intensity and vigor of her life of prayer, private and communal, balanced with a life connected to the natural world, balanced with a life of study, gave her *metanoia* process a sort of rarified formation. These embodied practices and disciplines strengthened and transformed her own capacities to think, to feel, and to will, though she started out in doubt. She was practical, but not utilitarian; she would have abhorred the corporate style in which every member of the work force is considered replaceable and interchangeable, like so many nuts and bolts. When she received a new postulant in her abbey, or when she lost a sister, she understood that each presence and each absence changed the entire dynamic of the communal organism. Last, Hildegard practiced self-knowledge in a very special creative way. She knew that her own downfall was pride, so in the *Ordo Virtutum,* the wonderful liturgical drama, she crowns Humility as the Queen of the Virtues! I bring that up, because it's a terrific example of *prescriptive thinking*, made audible in music. (Personal communication, 2008)

With only a thirty-five-year history, the work of music-thanatology is characterized by growth. The student profile calls men and women of great spiritual diversity (Christians, Jews, Buddhists) and employment histories (nurses, physicians, attorneys, musicians, social workers, teachers, pastors, pharmacists, etc.). There are forty-five to fifty-two students enrolled in the Chalice of Repose Project's online educational programs each year, with graduate students being placed as clinical interns at hospitals and hospices across the country. The same Oregon faculty is launching a new interdisciplinary master's degree in a collaborative effort with the Catholic University of America in Washington, D.C., where Schroeder-Sheker has been an artist and clinician in residence for several years. "All this growth, infused by strong, dedicated students!" she said. "I can't help but think of Hildegard's *viriditas.* We are definitely, in our own little way, experiencing the greening of tradition."

Woman: *Opus Dei*

It is quite obvious that contemporary women religious and women involved in religion are vitally interested in Hildegard of Bingen's relevance to the issue of gender and religious leadership in the church and theological academy today. It is not an overstatement to say that the place of women in ecclesiastical matters has vexed the church for millennia. As a comprehensive system, Western patriarchy took nearly fifteen hundred years to evolve. Literally meaning "the rule of the fathers," patriarchy is a historical phenomenon created by human beings with a consistently operating life span of four thousand years; hierarchically ordered, literally meaning "the rule of the holy" and militaristic in operational style, where some men control the power and resources and distribute them to some men and all women and children who are the rightful property of some elite ruling class men. Patriarchy was firmly established by 600 B.C.E. as the overarching explanatory system of Western civilization (Lerner 1986).

Through history and in principle, the church has not recognized female right to ecclesiastical jurisdiction except in matters pertaining to female religious life and then with severe limitation. Female subjugation was firmly entrenched by the time of the writing of the Hebrew scripture and carried into the world of the New Testament. By 90 C.E., the following appears in I Timothy 2:11–12, "Let a woman learn in silence with all submissiveness. I permit no woman to teach or to have authority over men; she is to keep silent." Augustine, Western Christendom's most influential theologian, provided the Western Fathers of the Church with the warrant to proclaim woman as "first in order of sin and second in order of creation."

While we are now consciously experiencing and exploring the implications of a post-patriarchal era, we are still in the spring season of the theological tasks facing the church today. In terms of anthropology, as Ruether notes, this means affirming that both men and women possess the fullness of human nature. There is no superior or inferior human nature; the male does not fulfill what lacks in female nature. Rather, woman as woman and man as man each possess the fullness of human nature as imprints of divine presence. Their relationship is of mutually transforming love that nurtures and empowers the full and equivalent human personhood of each (Ruether 1991, pp. 372–73). The work remains underway of reincorporating the importance of female prophecy and the role of women in the scriptural record, of revising theology and spirituality with the lights of gender inclusivity, with recovering the historical role of the medieval abbess and discerning its implications for religious life today, for exposing Hildegard's potent religious leadership and applying its daring to churchwomen in the third millennium of Christianity. When asked who inhabits the spirit of Hildegard of Bingen today, I reply: Sister Joan Chittister, OSB. Chittister is one of the most profound and prophetic voices in progressive Christianity today. She is another Benedictine woman, reformer, and leading voice for more than a quarter century on issues in church and society, human rights, peace and justice, and contemporary religious life and spirituality. Sister Chittister is presently executive director of the creative venture Benetvision: A Resource and Research Center for Contemporary Spirituality, internationally active lecturer, and author of thirty-five books.

Why is it that twelfth-century Benedictine abbess and multi-talented reformer Hildegard of Bingen, once eclipsed, has returned so forcefully into contemporary consciousness? One response is that she is a creative phenomenon. What has brought her back as such an imaginative force is her stunning multidimensional individuality. Emotionally, spiritually, and intellectually, Hildegard exercises an inventive freedom that links her to our time primarily because of the depth and scope of her expressiveness across so many venues of creativity.

Note

1. For information on Therese Schroeder-Sheker, her recordings or publications, or to read about the Chalice of Repose Project, see www.chaliceofrepose.org. Schroeder-Sheker's dynamic and prodigious career has been distinguished with over one hundred scholarly publications, five CD recordings, seven film scores, numerous awards and grants in medicine and the humanities, an Emmy, a gold record, a Christopher, a Palm Springs International Film Festival First Place, a Jerome, a Gabriel, and featured television documentaries in the United States (ABC, NBC, PBS, CNN) and Europe. She has founded large, all-city clinical practices serving thousands of patients and their families; chaired university, seminary, and college programs in music and pastoral theology, and delivered over one hundred and twenty-five plenary addresses to national and international congresses in medicine and/or the humanities.

Application

I have raised and explored seven reasons for the reemergence of twelfth-century Hildegard into contemporary consciousness:

1. Reviving the historical record of strong and creative women who have come before us so that we do not forget their existence and witness.

2. Respecting a vision of the interconnection of creation and humanity as composed of the same elements that must remain in harmony and in balance to experience healthy well-being—physically, spiritually, and cosmically.

3. Returning to the notion of virtues as cultivating the traits and ways of being that exemplify our better selves.

4. Taking seriously the role of the unconscious in human personality in order to strive for greater individuation and integration personally and collectively.

5. Awakening to the ecological crises prophetically named by Hildegard and now our global reality.

6. Retrieving the monastic beauty of contemplative musicianship as a healing art.

7. Celebrating the ever-ancient, ever-new story of women's religious leadership, especially in the dawn of a post-patriarchal era in the West.

Reflecting on these considerations, which of them resonate with your personal experience? How do they relate to what matters most for you?

Are there additional reasons as to why Hildegard has "returned" that you would add to the list? What makes them significant for today?

CHAPTER 3

Confrontation with the Unconscious

I stretch out my hand to God,
so that I am sustained and carried
ever so lightly
like a feather on the breath of God.

—Hildegard of Bingen, *Analecta Sacra*

Too few people have experienced
the divine image as the innermost possession
of their own souls.
Christ only meets them from without,
never from within the soul.

—C. G. Jung, *Psychology and Alchemy, par. 12*

It is a fearful thing to fall
into the hands of the living God.

—Letter to the Hebrews 10:31

In *Was C. G. Jung a Mystic?* Aniela Jaffé opens up Jung's understanding of God as mystery by quoting from Jesuit theologian Karl Rahner, who Jaffé believed expressed himself in similar ways to Jung: "Whoever does not love the mystery, does not know God; [s]he continually looks past [God] . . . and worships not [God] but the image of [God] made to our specifications" (Jaffé 1989, pp. 61–62).

God, for Jung, is transcendental mystery, the mystery of all mysteries (*Letters* 1, Dec. 31, 1949). This reference to Karl Rahner brought to mind a provocative, oft-quoted essay that Rahner wrote, titled "The Devout Christian of Tomorrow Will Be a Mystic." Rahner opined, "The devout Christian of the future will either be a mystic, one who has experienced something, or [s]he will cease to be anything at all" (1971, p. 15). Forty years ago, Rahner was talking about the plausibility of mature Christian faith in an era he described as a "wintry season." Further exploration reveals that Rahner, one of the most prolific and celebrated Catholic theologians of the twentieth century, actually was speaking not exclusively to Christians but to humanity in general in saying that the person of tomorrow will be a mystic or will cease to be. Similarly, not long before his death, Jung was asked if civilization would survive. He said it would if enough people began to take responsibility for their inner lives, for living consciously. Hildegard was saying the same thing eight hundred years earlier. They knew something that is now forcefully coming to consciousness: the final human frontier is the exploration of inner space. The inward quest is the relentless search for an experience of *Mysterium*. Interest in this experience and the language of spirituality is becoming increasingly important as a means of articulating how we understand the place and significance of transcendence in our lives.

> The final human frontier
> is the exploration of inner space.

Spirituality and Mysticism

While spirituality and mysticism are similar, they do not refer to identical realities. Spirituality is the more embracing term and can be understood in the context of this discussion to encompass the following:

> The daily lived aspect of one's faith commitment in terms
> of values and behaviors; how one appropriates beliefs about
> God and the world; the process of conscious integration and

transformation of one's life; the journey of self-transcendence; the depth dimension of all human experience; a dialectic that moves one from the inauthentic to the authentic and from the individual to the communal; the quest for ultimate value and meaning. (Dreyer and Burrows 2005, p. xv)

Mysticism refers to an encounter with, and experience of, what Rudolf Otto termed the *numinosum*. This term captures the reality that underlies all religions. Jung believed that religion, all religion in its essence, is the careful observation of the *numinosum*. Otto calls the mystical experience "numinous" and identifies three components of this transformational phenomenon: *mysterium tremendum et fascinans*. Using the Latin heightens the sense of the awesomeness of such an encounter with the "Wholly Other."

Elizabeth Johnson unpacks the meaning of the mystery that is at once awesome and attractive:

> *Mysterium* refers to the hidden character of the Holy, beyond imagination, laced with promise: more fullness exists than we can grasp.
>
> *Tremendum* denotes the awesome character of this mystery insofar as it is beyond control. We cannot domesticate the power of the Holy. This gives rise to a feeling of reverence akin to fear: we are so small in the face of this majesty.
>
> *Fascinans* expresses the attractive character of this mystery insofar as it is overwhelmingly gracious. Experienced as love, mercy, and comfort, the Holy makes us blissful, longing for this goodness: Holy is the power to entice and lure our hearts. (2008, pp. 8–9)

Mysticism explores the extraordinary experience of meeting Mystery and the response of "taking off one's shoes" as we realize we are in the presence of the Holy (Exodus 3:5). In addition, the numinous is also *tremendum* in that it prompts terror precisely because the power of the Holy is beyond human comprehension and control. It is indeed a fearful and terrifying thing to fall into the hands of the living God, as recorded in the biblical testimony of the Letter to the Hebrews 10:31. Lastly, the encounter with the Holy is immanently fascinating and humans are innately drawn in the direction of the sublime touch of God (Otto 1923).

"Praying"

It doesn't have to be
the blue iris, it could be
weeds in a vacant lot, or a few
small stones; just
pay attention, then patch

a few words together and don't try
to make them elaborate, this isn't
a contest but the doorway

into thanks, and a silence in which
another voice may speak.

—Mary Oliver, *Thirst*

Theologically speaking, since God's self-communication is ongoing and ever available, persons experience God in all arenas of life, from the mundane to the sublime, since, as Gerard Manley Hopkins notes, "The world is charged with the grandeur of God" (1952, p. 70). Human beings have experienced the numinous from time immemorial. Mysticism is part of spirituality; the spiritual life is radically mystical. There is a deep yearning within the human being, arising from the soul that seeks connection to Holy Mystery, which is experienced in the encounter with the numinous: *mysterium tremendum et fascinans*. Amazingly, this intimate, intense, extraordinary experience of God is alive in the domain of the everyday and available to everyone. This is why Rahner believed that everyone is invited into the possibility of the mystical directly through the experience of their living. In *Encounters with Silence*, first published in 1960, Rahner explored the notion—rooted in the spirituality of St. Ignatius of Loyola, the sixteenth-century founder of the Society of Jesus (Jesuits)—of finding God in all things. Rahner poignantly prayed to be receptive to finding the extraordinary in the ordinary when he titled a prayer "God of our daily drudge":

> I must live out the daily drudge and the day that is yours as one reality. As I turn outward to the world, I must turn inward toward you, and possess you, the only One, in everything. But how does my daily drudge become the day that is yours? My God, only through you. Only through you can I be an "inward" person. Only through you am I with you within myself even as I am turning outward in order to be among things . . . In your love, all turning outward to the daily drudge becomes a retreat into your unity . . . .
>
> But this love that lets the daily drudge be the daily drudge and yet transforms it into a day of recollection with you—this love only you can give me. What am I to say to you as I am bringing myself, the bedrudged into your presence?
>
> I can only stammer a request for your most commonplace of gifts, which is also your greatest: the gift of your love. Touch my heart with your grace. Let me, as I grasp after the things of this world in joy or in pain grasp and love *you* through them, you, the One beyond all graspness, the primordial ground of all. You, who are love, give me love; give me yourself, so that all my days may eventually flow into the one day of your eternal life. (2004, pp. 49–50)

Earth's crammed with heaven,
And every common bush afire with God;
But only [those] who see it take off [their] shoes—
The rest sit around and pluck blackberries.

—Elizabeth Barrett Browning, *Aurora Leigh*

Before exploring Hildegard's and Jung's experience of the numinous it is important to identify what each means by the Wholly Other or Holy Mystery—God. These distinctions will assist us in better adapting the insights of depth psychology to both the visionary insights of Hildegard and its meaning for those on the spiritual quest today. To begin with, Hildegard, as a representative of the long sweep of Christian mysticism, and Jung, as a modern person in search of the soul, would agree that the experience of the numinous is of biblical proportions, alive with a sense of *mysterium tremendum et fascinans* and utterly incomprehensible. God is simultaneously existentially present in human experience and unfathomable, the already not yet.

Hildegard's Spiritual Conditioning

Hildegard was strongly under the influences of the later Middle Ages of a Christianized Europe. Her spirituality was shaped by medieval Christian monasticism, biblically rooted in such disciplines as the *Lectio Divina*, Latin for "spiritual reading," which refers to the regular praying with the Holy Scriptures following the pattern of four movements: *lectio*, slow reading of the biblical text; *meditatio*, reflection upon the text; *oratio*, opening one's heart to God and entering into interior dialogue with God; and *contemplatio*, listening for God's response and opening oneself to living under the influence of God's directing Spirit. The way she interpreted her mystical experience of God must be understood through the lens of how she understood God through the biblical, philosophical, Catholic, and Benedictine traditions. It is not surprising that her interior visions, which form the basis of her illuminated manuscript *Scivias*, for example, are rich with imagery that suggest to her, under the influence of the Holy Spirit, a reformulation of such Christian doctrines as the Trinity and the Incarnation. She does not nor can she separate her experience and understanding of God from the Trinitarian God of Christianity.

Listen with the ears of your heart.

—Prologue to the Rule of St. Benedict

It is these symbols that mediate how she interprets and expresses her mysticism. Hildegard's lush, visionary interior life finds its roots and takes its wings from the God of Abraham and Sarah, Moses and Miriam, the Old Testament prophets, Mary, Jesus, Paul, Benedict, Augustine, and Aristotle, to name a few. Hildegard's novelty and creativity give witness to how one works with the phenomenon of "epiphany"—the mysterious and unexpected inbreaking of the numinous into the daily drudge of everyday life. Epiphanic vision is defined as a spiritual and imaginative experience, neither contrived nor anticipated, whose meaning can be discerned through methods such as those of *lectio divina*: study, meditation, prayer, and theological reflection. The overflow or product of this engagement is conversion, which leads to meaningful change in the way one lives one's life. Barbara Newman says, "The epiphanic vision is the mainstay of the medieval genre dominated by women" (2003, p. 300).

A Doctor of Souls

Above all, Carl Gustav Jung identified himself as an empirical scientist who embraced the conviction that "the world inside and outside ourselves rests on a transcendental background is as certain as our own existence" (1955–56, par. 787). In a letter to an unnamed recipient, Jung wrote: "You are quite right, the main interest of my work is not concerned with the treatment of neuroses, but rather with the approach to the numinous" (*Letters* 1, Aug. 20, 1945). Jung identifies numinous experiences as those that

> [hint] at an unseen presence, a numen to which neither human expectations nor the machinations of the will have given life. It lives of itself, and a shudder runs through the man who thought that "spirit" was merely what he believes, what he makes himself, what is said in books, or what people talk about. But when it happens spontaneously it is a spookish thing, and primitive fear seizes the naïve mind. (1954, par. 35)

For Jung, the psyche itself possesses a religious function: *anima naturaliter religiosa,* meaning the soul is naturally religious.[1] By nature, the human person is *homo mysticus.* Mystical experience is exceptional only in regard to its intensity, not in respect to its natural availability to human striving for union with God.

VOCATUS ATQUE NON VOCATUS DEUS ADERIT
("Summoned or not, God will be there")

—Motto carved above the door of Jung's house
in Küsnacht, near Zürich

. . . from my eleventh year I have been launched upon a single enterprise which is my "main business." My life has been permeated and held together by one idea and one goal: namely, to penetrate into the secret of the personality. Everything can be explained from this central point, and all my words relate to this one theme.

—C. G. Jung, *Memories, Dreams, Reflections,* p. 206

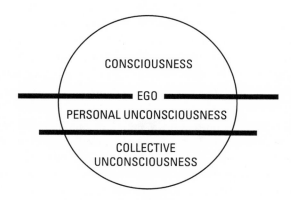

A diagram of Jungian psychology

His separation from his mentor Sigmund Freud was in part based on Jung's discovery that the contents of the unconscious in the human personality were far richer than as solely the repository of repression and sexuality. Jung became convinced that the unconscious was the bridge to the mystical, soul-full, dimension of the human personality. "From that moment on, Jung's concern became more and more a religious concern, however scientific and empiric the instruments chosen for the service. The unconscious was no longer a source of conflict and derangement but a world in which health and sanity and salvation had to be sought" (van der Post 1975, pp. 205–29). Important as it had been to discover and explore the unconscious in the interests of the mentally ill, Jung now recognized the contents of the unconscious as hosting life or death for the soul's journey to wholeness.

The Life of the Psyche

At this point, a brief foray into the meanings of the terms of Jungian psychology and how they function is helpful. The diagram provides a way to visualize what we are speaking about here. For Jung, the psyche—the whole of the human personality—contains conscious and unconscious components. In short, the upper structure of the psyche, the center of consciousness known as the ego, means our personality as we are aware of it and experience it firsthand. Stein says, "The ego is a kind of mirror in which the psyche can see itself and can become aware" (1998, p. 15). What we know about ourselves consciously, however, is only about one-tenth the total of our personality. The other nine-tenths of who we are finds its home in the unconscious dimension. Examine the extraordinary photo of an iceberg (plate 4) and this will help you visualize the scope and depth of the unconscious in relation to consciousness.

The hidden contents of the unconscious comprise not only repressed or dissociated memories but also ideas, images, stories, fantasies, and emotions yet to be brought to conscious awareness—including the ever-important personal and collective shadow. The unconscious is divided into a personal unconscious and a collective unconscious, where the archetypes find their home. Archetypes are innate imaginative potentials, primordial images, and ancient myths that inspire similar behavioral and emotional reactions and patterns in all people irrespective of culture, religion, or historical period. In this collective unconscious the same patterns never vary.

Since the reality of the dark dimension within the human personality is germane to the continued discussion of numinous experience, it is important to say something here about the meaning and function of the shadow, which will be discussed in more detail in the next chapter. The shadow contains the neglected qualities of the personality, consisting of partly repressed, partly unlived traits, that, for social, ethical, educational, or other reasons, have been excluded from conscious awareness. Some elements of the shadow can indeed be harmful, resulting in uncontrolled anger, impulsive sexuality, or other harmful behaviors that are dystonic to the person's conscious identity. In contrast, the arduous task of consciously facing shadow material, which is often blanketed by shame or guilt, may help to reveal human and spiritual potentiality.

The personal and the collective shadow are illustrative of the very one-sidedness that Jung found to be the source of so much neurosis. For example, gender conditioning shapes children to be one way and not another. Boys are taught to repress painful emotion by not crying (often resulting in acts of violence instead of the release of weeping), and girls are permitted tears but trained not to be too aggressive or assertive (often resulting in depression and acts of anger turned inward). Our psychic system, just like our body, seeks a universal sense of well-being—healing—whereby anything that is undernourished or underdeveloped naturally reaches for realignment in order to function with integrity, wholeness: balanced, interconnected, and integrated.

The Unconscious: Pathway to the Numinous

Encounter with the unconscious is the only available source of accessing the experience of the numinous. The unconscious is the medium from which deep religious experience springs. Connection to this *Mysterium* is humankind's best hope for healing the soul sickness and fragmenting forces battering the human psyche. In short, those within a religious tradition are prone to name the encounter with the *mysterium tremendum et fascinans* God, Yahweh, or Allah, for example, and those personality scientists, like Jung, call it the unconscious. When Jung spoke of God, he meant an experience in the psyche of an incomprehensible, autonomous, and unpredictable force. He said, "One must always remember that God is a mystery, and everything we say about it is said and believed by human beings. We conceive images and concepts, and when I speak of God I always mean the image man has made of Him. But no one knows what He is like unless he is a god himself" (Jaffé 1989, p. 61).

So Paul, standing in the middle of the Areopagus, said:
People of Athens, I perceive that in every way you are
religious. For as I passed along, and observed the objects
of your worship, I found also an altar with this inscription,
"To an unknown god." What therefore you worship as
unknown, this I proclaim to you.

The God who made the world and everything in it,
being Lord of heaven and earth, does not live in shrines
made by humans, nor is God served by human hands,
as though God needed anything, since God gives to all
people life and breath and everything . . . God is not far
from each one of us, for "in God we live and move
and have our being."

—Acts of the Apostles 17:22–28a

In other writings, Jung qualifies his identification of God with the unconscious by saying that the unconscious is not identical with God or set up in place of God. While Jung has been criticized for his "reduction" of God to a psychic factor, a thorough reading does not find that Jung conflates God with Self, the integrating center of the psyche. Mystics, like Hildegard and others within the long sweep of the faith of ancient Israel and the Christian tradition, speak of an encounter with God as an unmediated direct existential experience of coming into contact with God as God. This is possible because the Christian tradition holds that it is in God's nature to reveal Godself. God possesses a desire for ongoing self-disclosure in history to people. Jungian psychology understands this experience in the sense that "God" represents a word or designation for something incomprehensible. It is actually the archetype of the God-image that one encounters in the unconscious. This archetype within the unconscious, seemingly stirred to life by forces outside the person, is, at the same time, the eruption of the Self seeking its healing and wholeness within an experience that defies complete human comprehension and thus remains always the Unfathomable. Stein argues that Jung was sadly concerned that "too few people have experienced the divine image as the innermost possession of their own souls. Christ only meets them from without, never from within, the soul"(1985, p. 141).[2] Hildegard was an exception to this conviction, an exception Jung recognized in his own work.

Hildegard as a Medieval Visionary

What kind of visionary experience did Hildegard have? What was the etiology of her visions: physiological, pathological hallucination, divine intervention, or some combination of these factors, or beyond human comprehension? How did she interpret these experiences? Can people have such visions today?

The imaginative was a feature of late medieval culture. As previously noted, Hildegard was born on the cusp of the century. The period immediately preceding Hildegard, the Dark Ages, was a time when the natural and supernatural worlds were not divided. Hildegard was aware that the practice of seeing the divine in all nature was eroding. As the distance grew between the ordinary lives of the people and the clergy, who alone dispensed the necessary graces for salvation, there was a deepening sense of the vitality of the personal interior life. The soul and the inner life became the landscape for the discovery of the divine. Hers was an epoch of spiritual fervor and the extraordinary expansion of monastic life. The monastery provided girls and women safety, protection from unwanted arranged marriages and multiple pregnancies, and the possibility of an education, as well as artistic and literary expression. Barbara Newman says, "While most scholars today hold visions to be exceptional events, medieval visions were in some contexts not only encouraged but expected" (2003, p. 29). *Lectio divina*, devotional use of images and visualization techniques, contemplation on paintings, lengthy vigils without sleep, and various physical mortifications were all practices that fostered the condition and disposed the mind and heart for interior visionary experience.

It is important to note that the drive inward, especially for females, was in no small part due to the cultural, social, religious, and ecclesiastical arrangements that kept women from seeking outer positions of authority and power. The visionary or numinous experiences of medieval women religious served as an alternative to the authority of the priestly office from which they were denied admittance. Monks and nuns in Hildegard's era would have been keenly aware of the misogynist traditions inherited through Western religion and philosophy. Already within the first few centuries of Christianity, woman, "first in order of sin and second in order of creation," lacked autonomous *imago dei* and remained in need of male headship because of Eve's original sin.[3] It was commonplace in early Christian literature to deposit blame for the first sin as a situation that extended from Eve to all other women, forever. Tertullian, an important Christian writer from the North African city of Carthage, in his treatise *On the Dress of Women*, offered this dictum to a female audience the early years of the third century:

> Do you not know that each of you is an Eve? God's sentence on your gender lives even in our times, and so it is necessary that the guilt must also continue. *You* are the Devil's gateway; *you* are the unsealer of the forbidden tree; *you* are the first foresaker of the divine law; *you* are the one who persuaded him whom the Devil was not brave enough to approach. How easily *you* destroyed man, the image of God! Because of the death, which *you* brought upon us, even the Son of God had to die. (Clark 1983, pp. 38–39)

Although reinforced by the normative theological tradition that, *qua* women, they were not created in God's image, women writers such as Hildegard ignored the reproach (Bynum 1992, pp. 135, 155). Women have long been granted encouragement and respect for dedicated lives of prayer and even "permission" to be prophets. During her lifetime Hildegard was widely revered as the *prophetessa teutonica.*

Hildegard's Visionary Experience:
The *umbra viventis lucis*

An unusual child, Hildegard confided in Jutta, "When I was three years old, I saw an immense light that shook my soul; but, because of my youth, I could not externalize it" (Sur 1993, p. 26). Another translation interprets this as Hildegard saying, "I suppressed the visions in quiet obscurity" (Flanagan 1989, p. 210). This light within her soul she named the *umbra viventis lucis*: a spiritual inseeing and reflection of the Living Light, happening day or night, in full consciousness, and in multicolor brilliance accompanied by a "hearing within the soul":

> I do not hear them with my outward ears, nor do I perceive them by the thoughts of my own heart or by any combination of my five senses. I hear them in my soul alone while my outward eyes are open. I have thus never fallen prey to ecstasy in the visions, but see them wide awake, by day and by night. (Gottfried and Theodoric 1995, pp. 35–36)

In a letter Hildegard wrote in 1175 to the monk Guibert, who later became her secretary, she says:

> I am now more than seventy years old. But even in my infancy...I was possessed of this visionary gift in my soul, and it abides in me still up to the present day. In these visions my spirit rises, as God wills . . . I see . . . I do not hear with bodily ears, nor do I perceive with the cogitations of my heart or the evidence of my

five senses. I see them only in my spirit, with my eyes wide open, and thus I never suffer the defect of ecstasy in these visions. And, fully awake, I continue to see them day and night . . .Yet my body suffers ceaselessly, and I am racked by terrible pains . . . So far, however, God has sustained me.

The light that I see is not local or confined. It is far brighter than a lucent cloud through which the sun shines. And I can discern neither its height nor its length or breadth. This light I have named "the shadow of the Living Light," and just as the sun and moon and stars are reflected in water, so too are writings [meaning the Scriptures], words, virtues, and deeds of men reflected back from it.

Whatever I see or learn in this vision I retain for a long period of time, and store it away in my memory. And my seeing, hearing, and knowing are simultaneous, so that I learn and know at the same instant . . . But the constant infirmity I suffer sometimes makes me too weary to communicate the words and visions shown to me, but nevertheless when my spirit sees and tastes them, I am so transformed . . . that I consign all my sorrow and tribulation to oblivion. *(Letters,* vol. 2, pp. 23–24*)*

More will be said of her description of the visionary experience later, particularly because it is this self-reporting that Jung uses in discussing the role of mystical experience in coming to consciousness, which is simultaneously an experience of liberation and healing.

Hildegard always insists that her visions are not the result of ecstasy, meaning she does not experience the numinous as in a trancelike state or in emotional rapture but receives her visions in full consciousness, "with eyes wide open." Her visionary experience and consequent insights never altered her normal faculties; there was no dreamlike state, trance, or hallucination. In other writings, she stresses the uniqueness of this fully conscious visionary state so that it is clear that her mystical experience is not to be equated with ecstatic visionaries. Initially, Hildegard confided only in Jutta and her priest-counselor-confessor Volmar, later to become her secretary and trusted friend, in sharing the contents of her visionary life.

Hildegard remained silent as to the multicolor images and theological content of her visions for many decades. Then, at forty-three, Hildegard broke silence on her inner experience by saying she was "instructed" by the Living Light "to put her hand to writing" and "release the power and mystery of hidden and marvelous visions." This creative eruption of the soul was, in Hildegard's understanding, the direct activity of the Holy Spirit overshadowing her and disclosing through her. Therein, she depicts this by her inclusion of a self-portrait and personal declaration at the beginning of her major doctrinal and visionary work, the *Scivias.* (see plate 5). When she begins to put forth what was going on inside her, it is a great ten-year outpouring, giving birth to the *Scivias*, an illuminated manuscript of twenty-six visions with theological commentary addressing an array of Christian doctrine, including Divine Majesty, the Trinity, creation, the fall, Incarnation, sacraments, virtues, and the end of the world.

Three points are important to note here. First, Hildegard's self-silencing was due to the fear of not having her spiritual and intellectual experience taken seriously. Self-doubt, ecclesiastical reprisals, and potential ridicule and humiliation were all at play in Hildegard's self-silencing for so many years. Second, her visions are interconnected on three levels: her unique capacity to have them; how she experienced the visions; and the content of her experience; that is, all she sees and hears in the visionary experience (Dronke 1984, p. 146). Third, I am treating Hildegard's visionary experience as authentic encounters with Holy Mystery, explosions from the unconscious, *and* as carefully cultivated efforts to interpret her inner experience as containing messages of profound meaning beyond the personal.

This seeming paradox in Hildegard reveals a well-honed skill still required of inventive, influential, and savvy female originators today.

Self-minimization to Maximize
God's Message

As she released what she had held within for so long, Hildegard made sure it was understood that her inseeing and insights were not of her making but were a divine manifestation within her, directed to the church at large. She repeatedly referred to herself as *indocta femina forma*—unlearned—"poor little figure that I am," "only a little feather carried by the wind that carries her where it wills," "I, wretched and more than wretched, in my name of woman," "I am a poor little figure, and in myself I have neither health, nor power, nor courage, nor knowledge." While employing this device consistently, Hildegard was quite the opposite. She was in fact an inexhaustible individual of great erudition. She employed this device of minimization both to enhance her prophetic claim and to ensure a hearing from learned males who would never have taken seriously such theological and intellectual originality from a female, who, according to the Great Philosopher (meaning Aristotle) was "as it were an impotent male, for it is through a certain incapacity that the female is female" (Garry and Pearsall 1989, p. 112). Barbara Newman notes, "Without the indispensable claim to prophesy, Hildegard's career as a writer and preacher would have been unthinkable" (1998, p. 7).

Hildegard finds a place in the grand sweep of religious history that has long granted to women the capacity for interior visions and the potentiality for prophesy. Both manifestations require the person receiving the visions or the person announcing the prophetic message to be the vehicle and voice, never the originator of the content of the vision or message. Hildegard put a new twist on female prophesy in identifying her visionary life as one not steeped in subjective revelation about affective experiences of the divine—ecstasy—but visions rich with objective doctrinal, ethical, and scientific content directed at a corrupted hierarchy, negligent clergy, and failing leaders both secular and religious. In the opening of Vision II.1 of the *Scivias*, Hildegard wrote:

> And I heard from the Living Fire a voice speaking to me: "Oh, you are wretched dross and a female ignorant of any teaching

by earthly masters, unable to read books with philosophical understanding, but since you are touched by My light, whose fire kindles within you like a burning sun, declare, proclaim, and write these, My mysteries, which you see and hear in mystical vision." (*Secrets of God*, p. 19)

Hildegard worked boldly to minimize herself in order to maximize God's message. Yet it is clear from historical analysis that Hildegard learned and drew on her education, from the Bible and its commentaries, the Benedictine rule and spirituality, studies of the Fathers of the Church and their moral and exegetical works, philosophy, astrology, natural sciences, and music. The clear and careful self-deprecation we see in Hildegard is a relief of sorts, casting her against other intellectual geniuses. Such internal machinations are not evident in the treatises of Augustine or the biblical commentaries of Jerome or the exposition of mental genius of Thomas Aquinas. Such was not required of them. Their words were recorded as their words and assumed to be worthy in and of themselves for serious theological consideration and debate without the necessity of being tied to divine inspiration or prophesy. This seemingly paradoxical dynamic in Hildegard reveals a well honed and spiritually rooted skill that is still required of inventive, influential, and savvy female originators today.

We should be careful, then, not to read Hildegard's protestations of ignorance too literally (see Ahlgren in Cherewatuk and Wiethaus 1993, pp. 46–63). Her portrayal of herself as merely a transmitter of divine messages glosses over the scope of her creativity, as well as the power of her personal encounters with *mysterium tremendum et fascinans*. The dis-ease with her gifts was quite real as she struggled for acceptance within the patriarchal context of her time. Yet, one wonders where the "device of minimization" ends and her own originality begins; where Hildegard's intellectual acumen and fertile spiritual imagination are springs of her own creative insight and where the inspiration of "the Living Light" intervenes with words and images beyond the mind and heart of any human. The question is, of course, rhetorical since we shall have no definitive answer. What we do know is that there is no coming to consciousness without suffering the transformative process. It is to this suffering that we now turn our attention.

> There is no coming to consciousness
> without suffering the transformative process.

Sickness, Suffering, and Sanctity

In her time, as already noted, Hildegard's visions would have been considered exceptional, even gifted occurrences, but not pathological or abnormal. She consistently reported the pain associated with her visionary experiences, as well as the suffering she endured holding in the workings of her inner world. In this regard it is important to offer a critical distinction between pain and suffering. Pain is understood here as actual visceral feelings, the distressing and debilitating physical experience. Suffering is understood as the interior or emotional feelings that rise from loss of meaning, inner emptiness, or psychic misery. Therefore, it is possible to have enormous physical pain and not be suffering. This is true of those who find some meaning in their illness and work with and through the pain to experience and express surprising vitality and vibrancy. Then again, there are those with little diagnosable physical pain but who suffer terribly. This distinction may be somewhat subtle but helpful in examining the pain and suffering associated with engagement with the numinous, the experience of awakening into new levels of consciousness, which is, in Jungian terms, an encounter with the unconscious. It is not uncommon, especially for female mystics, and as in the case of Hildegard, for the visionary to experience both pain and suffering, *and* extraordinary feelings of well being associated with bringing the vision to fruition and integrating its insights. As Dronke states, "Hildegard did not simply suffer such disturbances: she made something imaginatively and spiritually fecund out of them" (1984, p. 147).

"Hildegard speaks so insistently and precisely of her physical symptoms, their duration, and her corresponding inner states," says Barbara Newman, "that modern scholars have felt confident enough to offer a diagnosis" (in Burnett and Dronke 1998, p. 197). Newman continues:

As early as 1917 Charles Singer, a historian of medicine, proposed that the abbess suffered from a form of migraine knows as "scintillating scotoma." That diagnosis was supported and popularized by the neurologist Oliver Sacks, and it has most recently been advanced by Hildegard's biographer, Sabina Flanagan, as the chief "explanation" not only for her visions but also for her assurance of divine inspiration. Flanagan posits that Hildegard experienced both common and classical migraines, including the celebrated migraine "auras" characterized by perceptions of shimmering light, fortresslike geometric figures, and most significantly, "feelings of sudden familiarity and certitude" like those sometimes experienced at the onset of an epileptic seizure. After her dramatic experience in 1141 [at age forty-three, when she "put her hand to writing" to "release the power and mystery of hidden and marvelous visions"], Flanagan argues, Hildegard came to interpret this sense of inner conviction as a call from God, and later still, she developed a conscious technique for utilizing her migraines in the service of her intellectual work. (Ibid., pp. 197–98)

Newman does not favor the one-to-one correspondence between her migraine episodes and visionary experience. It is far too mechanical an interpretation and an underestimation of the authenticity, intensity, and unpredictability of Hildegard's encounters with the numinous. It is interesting to note that Hildegard's symptoms and her interpretation of her pain and suffering changed as her life developed. Her awakening in her forties, her middle years, inaugurates a new way for her to experience the physical and spiritual happenings associated with her visionary life. Hildegard names the pain associated with her visions *pressura*—a term that conveys at once her sense of physical discomfort, as well as the suffering associated with the psychological pressure to break silence on her secret and the fears associated with confronting potential social disapproval and mockery (ibid., pp. 198–99). Hildegard works with and through the pain, which evolves into a condition less disabling; her suffering eases as she expresses the "numinous" sights and sounds arising from her visions.

I was afflicted till I named
the place where I am now.

—Hildegard, *Vita*, p. 49

It has become a necessity for me
to write down my early memories.
If I neglect to do so for a single
day, unpleasant physical symptoms
immediately follow.

—C. G. Jung, *Memories, Dreams, Reflections*, p. vi

When Hildegard had the vision that directed her to leave Disibodenberg and begin the construction of a monastery of her own, she experienced great pain and suffering, which foreshadowed the resistance she would receive from Abbot Kuno. He initially did indeed resist and then relented when he witnessed the paralysis and power that emanated from her sickbed. Hildegard reported that her physical pain and spiritual suffering was due to the fact that she "had not manifested the vision that was shown to me . . . that I should move" (*Vita* 2,5). Her debilitating symptoms evaporated each time she released what was inside her and worsened again each time she repressed or faced obstacles and resistances from others. Her *Vita* records her own words: that she was afflicted until she could name the place from which she was living. Only then did she recover her sight and regain energy. When she acceded to the Living Light, all weariness of body and heaviness of heart lifted, and she says, "all at once I feel like a simple young girl, and not like an old woman" (Schipperges 1997, p. 13).

In the relation of pathology to religion I have always followed James's dictum that religious experience should be judged by its "fruits and not its roots." If a pathological origin results in what Hildegard has left us, then I have no problem with it.

—John Dourley

The Numinous in the Guise of Pathology

The whole phenomenon of visionary experience fascinated Jung precisely because, eight centuries after Hildegard, he had come to believe that psychological neurosis and its manifestations in physical sickness arose from repression of "the story that is not told," the inner emptiness that arises from disconnection from meaning. The internal suffering and physical pain held some aspect of the numinous and could be healed if one allowed the contents of the unconscious to be raised to consciousness and taken into the self, the integrating center of one's being. Earlier mention was made of the letter sent to an inquirer in which Jung clarified,

> the main interest of my work is not concerned with the treatment of neurosis, but rather with the approach to the numinous. But the fact is that the approach to the numinous is the real therapy, and inasmuch as you attain to the numinous experience, you are released from the curse of pathology. Even the very disease takes on a numinous character. (*Letters* 1, Aug. 31, 1945, unnamed addressee)

This is a pivotal intersection for both Hildegard and Jung: *even the very disease takes on a numinous character.*

Two of the seven references Jung makes to Hildegard in his *Collected Works* have to do with interpreting the inner experience of the numinous. Jung says,

> The phenomenon itself, the vision of light, is an experience common to many mystics, and one that is undoubtedly of the greatest significance, because at all times and places it proves to be something unconditioned and absolute, a combination of supreme power and profound meaning. Hildegard of Bingen, an outstanding personality quite apart from her mysticism, writes in much the same way about her central vision:
>
>> Since my childhood I have always seen a light in my soul, but not with the outer eyes, nor through the thoughts of my heart; neither do the five outer senses take part in this vision. . . . The light I perceive is not of a local kind, but is much brighter than the cloud which supports the sun. I cannot distinguish height, breadth, or length in it. . . . What I see

> or learn in such a vision stays long in my memory. I see,
> hear, and know in the same moment. . . . I cannot recognize
> any sort of form in this light, although I sometimes see in
> it another light that is known to me as the living light. . . .
> While I am enjoying the spectacle of this light, all sadness
> and sorrow vanish from my memory.
>
> I myself know a few individuals who have had personal
> experience of this phenomenon. So far as I have been able
> to understand it, it seems to have to do with an acute state
> of consciousness, as intense as it is abstract, a "detached"
> consciousness, which, as Hildegard implies, brings into
> awareness areas of psychic happenings ordinarily covered
> in darkness. . . . As a rule, the phenomenon is spontaneous,
> coming and going on its own initiative. Its effect is astonishing
> in that it almost always brings about a solution of psychic
> complications and frees the inner personality from emotional
> and intellectual entanglements, thus creating a unity of being
> which is universally felt as "liberation." (1957, pars. 42–43)

Jung was impressed with Hildegard as a historical witness to the
fact that one can endure the pain and suffering of "coming into
the Living Light" via the "spookish" path of encounter with the
numinous and remain a whole personality, meaning not becoming
split, fragmented, or psychotic. Hildegard and Jung merge in the
conviction that suffering is an endemic part of the human, spiritual
experience; the only way to overcome it is to endure its darkness.
The unconscious in human personality yearns to be drawn into
the light, yet at the same time the forces of the ego and persona
will resist the often painful claims it places upon consciousness
to deal with the secrets within. Many persons pass through such
potentially transforming experiences but fail to stay with them long
enough to confront the inner turmoil and psychic suffering that
accompany the inbreaking of the divine in order to emerge with
greater wholeness of self and direction in life.

Jung's Confrontation with the Unconscious

By the time Jung was an adolescent, he felt isolated from others due
to his lushly imaginative inner life, which was of little interest to his

parents, relatives, and friends. Yet, Jung writes, "it never occurred to me that I might be crazy, for the light and darkness of God seemed to me facts that could be understood even though they opposed my feelings" (Stein 1985, p. 78). Jung's ability to stay with the "spookish," as he calls it, created the inner and outer condition of receptivity to withstand the encounter with the numinous: *mysterium tremendum et fascinans*. Jung experienced similar crises to Hildegard throughout his life: physically debilitating illness with severe inner disturbances followed by experiences of relief and restoration when he came to awareness of what it was he needed to express, which often occurred in symbolic formulation (paintings of mandalas, clarification of concepts, or articulation of new psychological theory).

The Uses of Sorrow

(In my sleep I dreamed this poem)

Someone I loved once gave me
a box full of darkness.

It took me years to understand
that this, too, was a gift.

—Mary Oliver, *Thirst*

At sixty-nine, in 1944, Jung had visionary experiences during a critical illness. At this time Jung's encounter with the unconscious subjected him to the devastating emotions of meeting the dark path to God—called in mystical spirituality the *via negativa* or dark night of the soul. The phenomenon of *la noche oscura*, literally from the Spanish meaning the dark or obscured night, finds its roots in the writings of sixteenth-century Spanish Carmelite reformers and mystics John of the Cross and Teresa of Avila, who illumine the painfully mysterious dark night that brings spiritual transformation (see May 2004 and Moore 2004). It is important to have a sense of this experience in order to appreciate what Jung encountered while in a weakened, vulnerable condition. According to this mystical tradition, it is not uncommon for those who live the examined life to find themselves in seasons where the path to well-being is obscured. Both Hildegard and Jung describe the dark night of the impending Living Light similar to the biblical Jacob wrestling through the night with the angel of God (Genesis 32:24–32). This wearying and terrifying sacred wrestle results in a radical kind of yielding to God that affects all the exterior and interior senses—it is the disposing of the whole self in relationship with *Mysterium*. It is a conversion experience whereby the sickness and suffering create the receptive, vulnerable, humble condition under which the unconscious erupts and consciousness is radically awakened; the road to the depths opens. Paradoxically, as both Jung and Hildegard report, the culmination of the process brings a sense of joy, contentment, clarity, humility, wholeness, and empowerment beyond words. To face the absolute unique giftedness of one's existence and accept its finitude creates the condition whereby one's consciousness can be awakened to the infinite.

All my writings may be considered tasks imposed from within; their source was a fateful compulsion. . . . I permitted the spirit that moved me to speak out. I have never counted on any strong response, any powerful resonance, to my writings. They represent a compensation for our times, and I have been impelled to say what no one wants to hear. For that reason, and especially at the beginning, I often felt utterly forlorn. I knew that what I said would be unwelcome, for it is difficult for people of our times to accept the counterweight to the conscious world. Today I can say that it is truly astonishing that I have had as much success as has been accorded me—far more than I ever could have expected.

—C. G. Jung, *Memories, Dreams, Reflections,* p. 222

Are Such Encounters with the Numinous Possible Today?

From both Christian and Jungian perspectives, it must be true that human beings can encounter the numinous in the here and now in radically imaginative and transformative ways. It is a transpersonal, transhistorical, and transcultural fact that human beings have experienced the numinous from time immemorial. Human beings possess an innate transcendental orientation and are, by nature, *homo mysticus*. As already stated, mystical experience is exceptional only in regard to its intensity, *not* in respect to its natural availability within the daily drudge—the human life span, however short or long. "Epiphanies"—the mysterious and unexpected inbreaking of the numinous into the ordinariness of daily living—remain a distinguishing feature of the unique ability of human beings to reflect upon their experience and plumb the depths of the unconscious, dark side where the contents of our souls are enwombed and awakened to deeper possibilities. The question is not whether spiritual visions are possible today, but why does such a potential seeded within each human being seem so fantastic, so out of the reach of regular folks that they deny the reality and relegate such happenings only to the saints of history and the Mother Teresas or Dalai Lamas of the modern and postmodern era? Far too many people approach the path to the depths but retreat, sabotaged by fear of the possible and the changes that such an encounter portends. They become depressed or fall sick in the understandable sidestepping of the deeper lure to wholeness and holiness.

Ancient Jewish Midrash tells the story that once a pagan asked a rabbi: "Why did God choose a bush from which to appear?" The rabbi responded: "Had God appeared in a carob tree or a sycamore, you would have asked me the same question. However, it would be wrong to let you go without a reply, so I will tell you why it was a bush: to teach you that no place is devoid of God's presence, not even a lowly bush" (Plaut 1981, p. 407).

I do a disservice to the content of this chapter, which seeks to explore a deeply mysterious phenomenon, by reducing it to merely inviting people today to be more aware and open; yet, at the same time, nothing is devoid of God's burning presence. Hildegard says, "You understand so little of what is around you because you do not use what is within you" (*Scivias* 1.2.29). Are we cultivating the spiritual imagination to see the burning bush outside our kitchen window, in the gaze of a lover, or the new green of spring following a long winter? By living with and in the darkness until the light dawns anew? When was the last time we sat silently, in absolute silence, listening?

Far too often we fearfully relegate to the shadow some of our most potent possibilities for living life to the full. Sometimes we strenuously resist the more noble feats of human becoming. Robert A. Johnson says, "To draw the skeletons out of the closet is relatively easy, but to own the gold in the shadow is terrifying" (1993, p. 8). The gold is related to the *imago Dei*—the image of God—each person carries within herself or himself. The gold is the encounter with *mysterium tremendum et fascinans* all around us waiting for us to notice and take off our shoes.

The second half of life and growing older were of primary interest to Jung. He said the afternoon of our life couldn't be lived by the morning's rhythm. Several months before Jung died, he wrote, "It is quite possible that we look at the world from the wrong side and that we might find the right answer by changing our point of view and looking at it from the other side, i.e., not from outside, but from inside" (*Letters*, Aug. 10, 1961). A crucial question he posed was, Are you related to something infinite or not?

Notes

1. Jung uses this Latin phrase as an interpretive spin on the ecclesiastical writer Tertullian's (160–225 C.E.) famous statement that the human soul is by nature Christian: *anima naturaliter christiana.*

2. Priest and paleontologist Pierre Teilhard de Chardin, SJ, once wrote: "One thing is definitely disappointing, I grant you: far too many Christians are insufficiently conscious of the 'divine' responsibilities of their lives, and live like other men, giving only half of themselves, never experiencing the spur or the intoxication of advancing God's kingdom in very domain of mankind" (1960, p. 69).

3. In his treatise *On the Holy Trinity*, St. Augustine, father of Western theology, said: "The woman together with her husband is in the image of God, so that the whole substance may be one image; but when she is referred to separately in her quality as helpmate, which regards the woman alone, then she is not in the image of God, as regards the man alone, his is the image of God as fully as when the woman, too, is joined with him." Sur quotes St. Augustine, "On the Trinity," commenting that the Augustinian theologian excuses the implication of Augustine's statement by arguing

that the quotation concerns only the bodily appearance (1993, p. 68). The facts of history disclose that this distinction has been missed by many and has had a direct bearing on the historical subordination of women's role in the church.

[My *raison d'etre* consists] in coming to terms with that indefinable Being we call "God."

—C. G. Jung, *Letters*, March 13, 1958

Application

Jung's Red Book

In a low period of his life, Jung began a self-experiment. He began a personal diary in words and illustrations in which he explored his inner experiences of the *mysterium tremendum et fascinans*. Although the *Red Book* has not yet been published for mass distribution as of this writing, portions of it—including the beautiful and vivid color drawings Jung used to record his experiences of God—are found in *C. G. Jung: Word and Image* (Jaffé 1979).* Jung "transcribed his inner experiences in the *Red Book*, a folio volume bound in red leather, which he richly illustrated. He painstakingly painted in the *art nouveau* style of the time, but he never regarded the paintings as art, only as an expression of what he was experiencing" (ibid., p. 66).

> Imagining your journal as a *Red Book*, allow an image of the infinite to emerge from within and release the image onto the page without self-consciousness or self-censure, but in free-flow form. For example, you may want to sit quietly in a favorite peaceful place to simply listen or choose an ordinary object in nature to contemplate in silence, while holding the question, "What am I noticing?" Just let what happens happen without thinking about it. Experiment with this exercise prior to moving into the next chapter, where the demonic and creative forces will be examined.

---

*The Philemon Foundation is working to complete funding for the editing of Jung's *Red Book*. Under "Works in Progress," the Foundation reports that this publication will be the most important since Jung's death and will inaugurate a new era in Jungian studies. The foundation is named for a central figure in the *Red Book*, an inner dialogue partner of superior insight (no connection to the Philemon in the Christian New Testament Letters of Paul). Jung says, "Philemon and other figures of my fantasies brought home to me the crucial insight that there are things in the psyche which I do not produce, but which produce themselves and have their own life" (1969, p. 183). For more information, see www.philemonfoundation.org.

Hildegard and Demons: The Interplay of Light and Shadow

If we remember that there are many people
who understand nothing at all about themselves,
we shall be less surprised at the realization
that there are also people who are utterly unaware
of their actual conflicts.

> —C. G. Jung, "New Paths in Psychology,"
> par. 425 (second edition)

Only when we connect misery to our cravings
can we begin to solve our dilemma.

> —Hildegard, *Scivias* 3.4.20

Spiritus contra Spiritum:
Spirit in Contrast with Spirits

In this chapter we explore the interplay of light and darkness, ego and shadow, virtue and vice, and the healing of the opposites in the journey to individuation through the lens of twelfth-century Hildegard of Bingen and twentieth-century Carl Gustav Jung.

There is an interesting connection between Carl Jung and the co-founder of Alcoholics Anonymous, Bill Wilson. Alcoholism, as many are aware, is "an illness which only a spiritual experience will conquer," as noted in the *Big Book* of Alcoholics Anonymous (1939,

p. 44). Bill Wilson credits this insight, the bedrock of recovery from alcoholism, to Jung. Jung had come to this conclusion after trying to help many alcoholics and seeing only a few of them recover, usually after just such an experience. In the 1930s, Jung was working with a patient named Rowland H. whose alcoholism was the equivalent of a slow suicide. Jung told Rowland H. that the progression of his alcoholism was hopeless without some type of spiritual conversion experience. This conversation took place after a year of psychoanalysis, during which Jung hoped to uncover and heal the destructive cycle of Rowland's drinking. Rowland achieved a brief period of sobriety with the help of Jung, only to relapse into intoxication again, which drove him to a depth of surrender and craving for release never experienced before. Rowland did indeed experience an encounter with the numinous, a spiritual conversion, which led him to join the Oxford Group, an evangelical movement dedicated to the principles of self-examination, confession, restitution, and service to others, where he met Ebby T., an old drinking buddy of Bill Wilson's. With Rowland's help, Ebby proceeded to get sober and, in turn, carried the message to Bill, who got the idea to apply the wisdom from these men to his own sobriety and eventually to the foundation of the Alcoholics Anonymous twelve-step program of recovery from addiction.

In January 1961, Bill Wilson wrote to Carl Jung to thank him for the unsuspecting role he played in the foundation of Alcoholics Anonymous. In this letter, Wilson recounts Rowland's story and the impact Jung had on him: "When he then asked you if there was any hope, you told him that there might be, provided he could become the subject of a spiritual or religious experience—in short, a genuine conversion" (Wilson 1987, pp. 68–69). Wilson continued to recount how Jung recommended that if such an experience were to happen to him and in him, he needed to place himself in some kind of religious atmosphere. Rowland's entry into the European Oxford Group provided him the external discipline of rigorous self-examination, honest confession, the activity of making amends for his past behavior, meditation, and prayer. Wilson's carefully composed and substantive letter included the story of his own descent into the hell of addiction, its despair, and the possibility of release if he, too, could follow the path that Jung had suggested.

He stopped drinking and did all he could to follow the Oxford Group formulas, and soon he had an experience of "illumination of enormous impact and dimension . . . my release from the alcohol obsessions was immediate. At once, I knew I was a free man" (ibid., p. 70). Wilson tells Jung that the spiritual experience brought with it a vision of a society of alcoholics, each identifying with and transmitting the experience to the next suffering person, creating a chain reaction of support and hope. He ends his letter to Jung with "Please be certain that your place in the affection, and in the history, of our Fellowship is like no other" (ibid.).

Jung's Foundational Insight: The Thirst for Wholeness

In Jung's reply, dated June 30, he told Wilson that he had often wondered what had happened to Rowland and was grateful to know the positive and generative outcomes of his spiritual conversion. He also told Wilson a few things that he had not told Rowland due to the fact that, at that time, he felt his notions about spirituality were "misunderstood in every possible way" by the traditional medical and psychoanalytic establishment: that he believed Rowland's "craving for alcohol was the equivalent, on a low level, of the spiritual thirst of our being for wholeness; expressed in the medieval language: the union with God" (Wilson 1987, p. 71). Jung asked, "How could one formulate such an insight in a language that is not misunderstood in our days?" (ibid.) Jung shared with Wilson the ideas that one embarks upon the path to greater freedom and integration through the inbreaking of unmerited grace, through honest mutual transformation of human relationships, or through the pursuit of a kind of knowledge and self-knowledge that goes beyond the confines of mere rationalism. Jung proceeded to express his conviction that the "evil principle prevailing in this world leads the unrecognized spiritual need into perdition if not counteracted either by real religious insight or by the protective wall of human community" (ibid.).

Jung understood that encounters with the depth and illuminating insights that lead to growth require the environment, the human/

numinous container, if you will, that religion, symbols, myth, and the human community necessarily provide to those choosing the narrow way that leads to life (Matthew 7:13–14). He concluded his letter by saying, "You see, 'alcohol' in Latin is *spiritus*, and you use the same word for the highest religious experience as well as for the most depraving poison. The helpful formula therefore is: *spiritus contra spiritum*" (Wilson 1987, p. 71). He meant by this that if the encounter and embrace of, and yielding to, the Spirit is going to take place, it will do so in an inner struggle within the individual against the antispiritual forces, which pummel the soul and seek its destruction.

Jung's experience with psychic suffering supported his strong intuitive sense that the human body and psyche could neither withstand such pressures nor heal without a reconnection to soul, the spiritual principle of human beings: the real, mystical dimension of the human being that contains the faculty for relation with the mystery at the depth of self, the center of the psyche. Jung's struggle with the Christian religion to provide such an environment of healing was, from his point of view, due to Christianity's failure to educate persons in the psychic reality of the life of the soul, thereby failing "to cure the soul of its tendencies to split and fragment" (Stein 1985, p. 141).

The ability to tell and own all of one's life story is essential to healing. The process of coming toward wholeness or integration belongs, according to Jung, to the work of the second half of life. Interestingly, this tenet of modern psychoanalysis is at the heart of a typical A.A. meeting. Neurosis thrives on psychological one-sidedness, a focus on *persona*—that face or mask you are willing to own and show to the world—to the exclusion of the more authentic, even darker, aspects of one's identity. The denial of the contents of the unconscious, the shadow material of one's life, leads to a one-sidedness that eventually puts life in tilt. As previously considered, "the shadow is made up of the personality's tendencies, motives, and traits that a person considers shameful for one reason or another and seeks to suppress or actually represses unconsciously" (Stein, ed., 1996, p. 17). The solution is a confrontation with the unconscious, a reorientation and restructuring from within, which integrates the opposites that had formerly been unreconciled (Stein

1985, p. 60). Jung's experience with those trapped in the vicious cycle of addiction, whose quest to be freed from its imprisonment was sincere and courageous, is illustrative of the process we all must endure in order to achieve our potential for self-realization.

Only when the dark side takes its place beside the light, the will to destroy beside the urge to create, terror beside love, and the world-opposites are seen together in a single image of God, only then does this picture fulfill the requirement of totality.

—Jacob Boehme, 1575–1624 CE

Individuation

Everything living dreams of individuation, for everything strives towards its own wholeness.

—C. G. Jung, *Letters* 2, April 23, 1949

At this point, it is important to acknowledge one of Jung's central convictions about human potentiality. The Self possesses an energy that is "manifested in the almost irresistible compulsion and urge to *become what one is*" (1950a, par. 634). Individuation is the innate impulse within the personality toward growth; an evolved individuality. It is important to understand that individuation is not the same as idiosyncratic traits that combine to make a personality unique. For Jung, individuation is understood as bringing together all conscious and unconscious contents—biological, social, cultural, psychological, and spiritual (Skelton 2006, p. 234).

Jung was convinced that every person encounters the demands of individuation. These demands are myriad, morally challenging, and threatening to established patterns of attitude and behavior, and they claim a goodly part of a lifetime of tough inner work and discipline to produce results. This lifelong process of integration, never fully accomplished in a lifetime, is conducted through the treacherous and deeply satisfying reconciliation of opposites within oneself. The psyche is inherently programmed to develop toward maturation. As such, individuation is an ethical statement about the natural goal of all life: the unfolding of what one is intended to be (Skelton 2006, p. 235). The maturational program can be thwarted—and most likely will be—distorted to the extent that life is not necessarily homeostatic, just, or easy.

[There is] a centre of personality, a kind of central point within the psyche, to which everything is related, by which everything is arranged, and which is itself a source of energy. The energy of the central point is manifested in the almost irresistible compulsion and urge to *become what one is* . . . .

—C. G. Jung, "Concerning Mandala Symbolism," par. 634

Concerning Mandalas: Symbol of Wholeness

Jung appeals to one of Hildegard's illuminations from the *Book of Divine Works* (see plate 6) when making the very point high-lighted in the box above.[1] In a section called "Concerning the Mandala Symbolism," Jung explores the meaning of the mandala, a Sanskrit word meaning *circle*. Jung says,

There are innumerable variants of the motif shown here, but they all are based on the squaring of a circle. Their basic motif is the premonition of a centre of personality . . .

This picture, from a manuscript of Hildegard of Bingen, shows the earth surrounded by the ocean, realm of air, and starry heaven. The actual globe of the earth in the centre is divided into four. . . .

They express the idea of a safe refuge, of inner reconciliation and wholeness. (1950a, pars. 634, 703, 710)

Jung notes he could have produced many more pictures from all parts of the world, but what would be true of all—as of the fifty-four different images—is that the same or very similar symbols are produced at all times, in all places, and among people of enormous diversity. Transconsciousness is born through the collective unconscious. Hildegard creates a mandala with no conscious awareness that mandala forms exist in Tibetan Buddhism or Dervish monasteries. This is the action of the archetypes. Of this Jung says, "And when we penetrate a little more deeply below the surface of the psyche, we come upon historical layers which are not just dead dust, but alive and continuously active in everyone—maybe to a degree that we cannot imagine in the present state of our knowledge" (ibid., par. 712).

This mandala shows, then, the union of all
opposites, and is embedded between *yang*
and *yin*, heaven and earth; the state of
everlasting balance and immutable duration.

—C. G. Jung, "Concerning Mandala Symbolism," par. 637

This is catholic thinking. This is the essence of "religious" thinking if we unpack the essential meaning of religion as *religare*, from the Latin, to heal separations, to bring together into a meaningful whole. The twelve steps of Alcoholics Anonymous set forth a pattern of self-critical examination, meditation, and action that, taken together, form a whole. The experience of recovery is predicated upon attention to the soul sickness that seeks healing through the "working of a program" within the environment of the safe refuge of meetings that ultimately produces inner reconciliation and a more anchored sense of wholeness. The steps themselves "function as instruments of meditation, concentration, and self-immersion, for the purpose of realizing inner experience" (Jung 1950a, par. 710). We are prompted to wonder, however, why it is that there is so much addiction within "developed" societies in the twenty-first century? We know there is no such thing as a static personality, yet many seem to remain compliantly in an almost fixed state. Why? Why is individuating such a minefield that it threatens to unravel our urge to become whole? Why is it that so many people are suffering from a refusal of the fact that they are essentially impelled toward growth and change?

The addiction keeps a person in touch with the god . . . the god comes in through the wound.

—Marion Woodman, "Worshipping Illusions"

Yearning for Unity and Union

It is not surprising that such a journey toward integrity is an arduous, confusing, and conflictual venture. So much of the inner world, the realm of the spirits, has been posed to us as far beyond the capacities of the average person due to the fallen human condition. In spite of so much human progress a rather pejorative view of humanity's goodness and potential prevails. Thus far we have spoken of the natural, innate transcendental orientation of the human person toward encounter and relationship with the numinous, God: Center and Source of human wholeness. One naturally asks the question that if humans are naturally oriented toward becoming whole, why is the process so wrought with tension and trouble? Why do we so readily turn to remedies outside ourselves for relief through such addictive avenues as drugs, food, gambling, materialism, and technology?

One answer is found in the ancient, centuries-old philosophy of dualism that underpins much of the Western worldview and whose vestiges continue to impact our assumptions about being an accomplished individual. The term *dualism* (from the Latin *duo,* meaning "two") has a variety of uses in the history of thought. In general, the idea is that there are two fundamental kinds or categories of things or principles. In theology, for example, a "dualist" is someone who believes that Good and Evil—or God and the Devil—are independent and more or less equal, competing forces in the world. Dualism contrasts with monism, which is the theory that there is only one fundamental kind, category of thing, or principle. Pluralism is the view that there are many kinds or categories. Dualism is the theory that the mental and the physical—

or mind and body—are, in some sense, radically different kinds of things that exist in contrast to instead of harmony with each other.

It was not until the great philosopher Aristotle (384–322 BCE) that the realities identified in the list of opposites (see p. 91) were understood as being in hostile opposition to one another. One side of the dualistic structure was overvalued, while the other side was undervalued, each placed in negative opposition to the other. Over centuries, the acceptance and integration of this mental framework left Western culture with a distain for the bodily, matter, nature, darkness, the emotional, and the feminine, for example. By Hildegard's time, this construct was fully articulated in theological, philosophical, and scientific theory. Male and female were hostile opposites and asymmetrically valued as intellect/body, active/passive, rational/irrational, reason/emotion, self-control/lust, judgment/mercy, and order/disorder. Thus, the superior, more rational, and spiritual dimensions of the human experience are developed through the elimination or repression of their "God-given" opposites. Furthermore, in recent times, with the shrinking of the world, expanding appreciation for interfaith and indigenous religious awakenings, and the advent of rapid communication systems, the gulf between Eastern and Western philosophy is diminishing. But while dualistic assumptions are gradually eroding, the dualistic mindset reducing the manifold aspects and dimensions of consciousness to opposing principles, such as spirit and matter, continues to impede the flow of an emergent Western twenty-first-century synthesis, whose roots find nourishing soil in both twelfth-century Hildegard and twentieth-century C. G. Jung.

Body and Soul: A Single Consciousness

Hildegard proposed a holistic vision of life, which provided an appealing counterpoint to the dualism so pervasive in her time. Women's inherent inferiority was taken for granted. This is the tradition that shaped Hildegard and she accepted it as the natural and hierarchical ordering of creation, but at the same time, she theorized and prophesized a different worldview. Hildegard envisioned the mutual interdependency, a sense of the partnership,

PHILOSOPHICAL SCHEME OF DUALISM

soul	body
spirit	flesh
sacred	secular
holy	profane
cognitive	intuitive
rational	emotional
mind	matter
grace	nature/sin
active	passive
strong	weak
authority	obedience
good	evil
light	dark
master	slave
masculine	feminine
man	woman

of body and soul. In this regard, she stands apart from the dualistic philosophical tradition in which she was trained, whereby the soul and body were to be viewed as hostile opposites. In the *Book of Divine Works,* she says, "It is the soul's joy to become effective in the body" (1987, pp. 95–96). In a letter addressed to the prelates in Mainz, and later in a sermon she delivered in her seventies, she explicitly addresses the dualist error and speaks to the oneness of the soul and body "existing in a single consciousness and single perfection":

> Happy indeed is the human whom God has conceived as a
> tabernacle of wisdom with the sensuality of his five senses . . .
> Body and soul are one with their particular powers and
> their name, as are flesh and blood; and by these three,
> namely by body and soul and by rationality, a human is
> completed and produces works. (Pernoud 1998, pp. 155–
> 56)

In another illumination from the *Book of Divine Works*, the last of her visionary trilogy and considered the most mature (II: 1, p. 23), we can appreciate her vision of humanity in relation to the cosmos, and her sense of the interdependency and interconnectedness of, as she calls it, the "web of all life" (see plate 7). This image is reminiscent of Leonardo da Vinci's great etching. Medieval historian Pernoud says:

> More than three centuries before his birth, this vision
> of man, arms extended over the globe of the earth, was
> present in the work of the little nun from the banks of
> the Rhine. But while Leonardo da Vinci has been studied,
> explored, extolled, and widely diffused in classic and
> modern times, the work of Hildegard and her era in general
> has been forgotten and unrecognized. The fact remains
> that his image, which places man in the center of the uni-
> verse, was familiar since the twelfth century and sum-
> marized what Hildegard reveals to us about the cosmos.
> (1998, p. 92)

Observe something else very important about both illuminations from the *Book of Divine Works:* Hildegard appears to have directed the placement of herself in the lower left-hand corner. In this extremely complex vision, Hildegard, in a bold and daring move, identifies herself as its inspired author. This miniature image within the larger image appears in a number of her illuminations. In interpreting this curious inclusion, historian Gerda Lerner says, "In the left-hand corner there is the figure of a seated nun, writing on two tablets. Her face is lifted up and touched by some sort of radiance. This self-conscious self-representation may very well be the first of its kind for a woman" (Lerner 1993, p. 64). Her self-visualization and articulation supports a view of Hildegard foreshadowing Jung in her clear claim of an individuating self.

Returning to Hildegard's illumination of the human in the center of the cosmos, there appears to be a person with three heads and four wings painted in shades of scarlet. The image is accompanied by pages of complex commentary about the symbolic meaning of the heads, faces, winged creatures, and assorted monsters. Hildegard records God's speaking to make sure that it was understood that God decides on every reality. From the beginning God wanted to create humanity to share the fashioning of the created universe. "Eternity is in the Father, the Word is the Son; the breath that binds the two is the Holy Spirit. God has represented it in man; man indeed has a body, a soul, and an intellect." Man is a reflection of the triple energy of God's love. Humanity is at the center of the world, in all its energy and array, alive in the midst of a dynamic universe. After expounding on the interconnectedness of all aspects of creation, as well as the sun, the moon, planets, and winds, Hildegard offered a further reflection on the human being when she says, "As for you, man, who see this spectacle, understand that these phenomena likewise concern the interior of the soul" (Pernoud 1998, pp. 99–100). This vision deals with a cosmic unity and interplay of all the elements of the created world and how all comes to bear on both humanity and the universe as organically connected. Thus the human being exists as a unitary work. Hildegard writes:

> We understand this unitary *opus* when we see how the soul brings air to its bodily organism through its thought processes. It brings warmth through every power of concentration; it brings fire through the intake of matter; in addition, it brings water by incorporating water materials and greening power through the process of procreation. And we humans are put together in this way the first moment of creation. Up above and down below, on the outside as well as on the inside, and everywhere—we exist as corporeal beings. And this is our essence. (Schipperges 1997, p. 39)

Hildegard's worldview was basically therapeutic: humanity-in-creation has the purpose and mission of being healed and saved and, in turn, of healing and saving. For Hildegard, such an enterprise was mediated through the gift of Christ. The Word (meaning God made flesh in Jesus Christ) linked the cosmos to the history of salvation through the bridge of the humanity of Jesus. Humanity embraced heaven and the earth and all created things within itself. God made humanity from the same stuff as the cosmos. By adhering to her anthropological cosmological worldview, Hildegard struck a balance between a strictly biological determinism and an exaggerated spiritualism. She developed an eco-theological worldview in which "the microcosm reveals the macrocosm, and all of history was seen as salvation history" (Craine 1997, p. 29). She theologizes on the interplay of microcosm and macrocosm. The human being is the centerpoint of God's creation; the mirror through which the splendor of the macrocosm is reflected. Her integrated vision melted the rigid boundaries imposed by the dualism that underpinned Western philosophy.

At sixty, she undertook the first of four preaching tours, yet again exceptional behavior for a medieval religious woman. She preached in cathedrals and town squares, to clergy and lay folk alike, against the dualist threat of the Cathars, and she scolded clergy for their infidelities to the true gospel. It is important to note that although Hildegard lived in near seclusion for most of her life, she was nonetheless aware of the problems of her times. She listened to the concerns of the laity as they sought counsel through the anchorage window. In her lovely portrayal of Hildegard, artist Cynthia Large attempts to capture this sense of Hildegard (plate 1). While she lived within the physical confines of a small cell on Mount Disibodenberg, she is available to those who come to her window to seek her healing ministries. Large's artistic rendering is bathed in light and reveals Hildegard with her hands raised in the gesture of healing blessing as the people gaze and lean in toward her. Hildegard's awareness of the troubles people endure and the conflicts in the world and church around her provided material for her powerful and provocative sermons.

Following her first preaching tour, in 1163, she completed the *Book of Life's Merits* or the *Book of the Rewards of Life (Liber Vitae Meritorum)*, whose six visions are all variations on the vision of the cosmic human being superimposed on the world. The text presented an animated symbolic conversation between thirty-five virtues with their attendant vices (see the table on p. 37). Instruction was also provided about penance, confession, purgatory, and the afterlife. Interestingly, she composed this text at the beginning of the eighteen-year-long schism between the papacy and Frederick I and the reign of the first antipope. No doubt the conflicts and destructive dynamics of her time influenced her desire to create this handbook for moral living.

The *Liber Vitae Meritorum* covers a total of thirty-five vices and outlines the punishment and penance for each. According to Sabina Flanagan, little prominence is given to the virtues, possibly because they were described in some detail in *Scivias*. The scope of the vices suggests a realization that their lure is hardly confined to the life of her nuns and thus reflects Hildegard's tendency for inclusiveness. Flanagan notes that some of the vices depicted, however, such as *tristitia saeculi* (worldly sadness or melancholy), are mentioned in the *The Life of the Holy Hildegard (Vita Sanctae Hildegardis)* as afflicting some of Hildegard's nuns. The vice is described in the *Liber Vitae Meritorum* (Part V: 35):

> I saw a fifth image in the form of a woman at whose back a tree was standing, wholly dried up and without leaves and by whose branches the woman was embraced. For one branch went around the top of her head, and another her neck and throat and one round her left arm and one to her right; her arms were not outstretched but held close to her body with her hands hanging down from the branches . . . Her feet were of wood. She had no other clothes but the branches going around her . . . And wicked spirits coming with a very fetid black cloud swarmed over her, at which she lay down lamenting.

Flanagan interprets the illumination suggesting the figure's attributes serve to emphasize the paralyzing effects of the vice. "The sense of apathy and inability to turn either to the world or to God makes the condition sound rather like what today might be called clinical depression," Flanagan speculates.[2] She continues her interpretation by saying:

The dry and lifeless tree (the symbolic opposite of all natural
vitality and spiritual growth) oppresses the mind of the sufferer,
preventing contrition. It constrains the neck and throat, thus
preventing the assumption of the Lord's yoke or nourishment
with the Food of Life. The branches hold the arms close to the
body so they cannot be extended in the performance of secular
or spiritual works. (1995)

The blocklike feet indicate that such people do not follow the
path of faith or hope. "There is no greenness in their ways," as
Hildegard puts it, using one of her favorite concepts, *viriditas*, the
green life force. Finally, the figure is naked because "it has no glory
or goodness to adorn it." The evil spirits are to be taken literally,
rather than symbolically; Hildegard believed in their existence and
thought that evil forces gained advantage of people by manipulating
them from within. Flanagan's interpretation of Hildegard's deep
understanding of the death-dealing forces provides apt illustration
of how very real the lure and power of unaddressed and unredressed
vice was for Hildegard. It does not diminish or demean convictions
about the essential goodness of human nature to accept equally
the devilishness within. In this regard, Jung would appreciate
Hildegard's psychological awareness of the malicious potentiality
of the unconscious and the capability for destructiveness if not
acknowledged intelligently. Hildegard, like Jung, believed that
inner harmony could be achieved, albeit partially, but not without
coming to consciousness through conflict.

Deliver Us from Evil

Hildegard wove a drama of the battle between good and evil in
human personality drawing on the thirty-five dialogues between
virtues and vices. This became the first morality play, called the
Ordo virtutum (*Play of the Virtues*, also translated as *The Play of
Forces*). The *Ordo Virtutum* predates other liturgical morality plays
by two hundred years. She is the first to use allegory in drama,
yet another example of Hildegard's creative daring as a medieval
religious woman crossing into the usual province of men. All the

characters in the *Ordo virtutum* are personifications: there is the heroine Anima, her companion Souls, and a villain, Diabolus. Hildegard works with sixteen of the virtues that resist the cunning, baffling, and powerful Diabolus.

As previously noted, Hildegard conceived of virtues as more than human habits, as creative forces within the cosmos as well as within the human soul. Without them, chaos reigns. *Ordo virtutum* was first performed in 1152 at her abbey at Rupertsburg, with roles taken by her twenty nuns and one male, possibly her secretary Volmar, who had the role of Diabolus. He never sings, only speaks, and does so with strident, unnerving shouting. While the *Scivias* pursued the exploration of the dynamic of the triumph of virtue over vice in human life, her *Book of Life's Merits* probed the dynamism of the inner struggle of good and evil spiritual forces within the Self/soul. It is Hildegard's main concern that human beings accept responsibility for the exercise of freedom in order to fulfill our unique destiny of living in and living as God's image. The ensuing conflict is an inevitable part of the process of achieving spiritual integrity. This can only be accomplished by a commitment to personal accountability for the development of a consciousness that faces into the reality of the power of the forces of light and darkness that are endemic in the human personality. At a key point in the drama the virtues lift Anima high into the air to signify she has gained sufficient strength to defy Diabolus as she sings: "Now, you trickster, I'll fight you face to face" (Dronke 1994, p. 151).

Hildegard possesses an almost uncanny awareness of the power of evil being as present in the spiritual life as the reality of God's bountiful grace. This may be due to growing up within the era of brutal Crusades, which she opposed, waged in the name of the Christian God, the growing corruption of the institutional church, and her conviction that its priests were failing to provide authentic sacramental and spiritual nurture for the people. In addition, as noted, she listened to and counseled countless people who sought her wisdom and knew well the medical, spiritual, sexual, familial, and economic predicaments of ordinary folks. While Hildegard was outspoken regarding various heretical groups of her time, such as the Cathars, and initially experienced such groups as manifesting the Antichrist, in her latter years she experienced the forces of the

Antichrist as being within the ecclesial system and embodied in actual lives of the custodians of that tradition. Evil and its symbolic agent, Diabolus (Satan), form a central feature of the Christian religious experience. Evil was no stranger to Hildegard and her *Book of Life's Merits* and *Play of the Forces* discloses the demonic forces as arising from within.

Conclusion

Speaking more psychologically than theologically, Hildegard, I believe, would conspire to a certain extent with Jung in accepting the reality that the forces of good and evil must be ultimately reconciled (Stein, ed., 1996, pp. 15–16). Hildegard never theologized, as did Jung, about the shadow in God but she certainly was convinced about the close proximity of the spiritual energies or forces.[3] For Jung, good needs evil in order to exist and each comes into being by contrast with the other (ibid.). The forces carry value-laden dissimilarity and must be harmonized, not denied, avoided, or projected out from one person to another, to other cultures, or the world stage. Hildegard in the twelfth century and Jung in the twentieth both decried humanity's failure to take evil seriously, which resulted in enormous corruption and violence. Such unconsciousness, then, insists that the evils besetting the human experience arise from sources other than ourselves. Both Hildegard and Jung shared a conviction that devilry inhabits the self. Accepting the reality of evil is actually a far more optimistic vision of human nature than relegating it to some objective force outside ourselves of which we have no control—"the devil made me do it" mentality. Since both Hildegard and Jung would agree that the essence of human nature is not evil but contains its possibility, it follows that hope reigns for humans to exercise their freedom in the direction of owning their shadows and striving to be receptive to personal/collective conversion and spiritual transformation.

We cannot escape the dark side of who we are, but as Jungian psychologist Robert Johnson says, we can play it out intelligently: meaning, take responsibility for it and do conscious work on it instead of laying it on someone or something else (1993, p. 15).

When we fail to do our own shadow work, we inevitably project a certain righteous indignation outward onto others, attacking them because we perceive in them the unattended shadow within ourselves (Stein, ed., 1996, p.17). Projection manifests itself in the form of excessive anger, vengeful thinking and acting, scapegoating, blaming, cruelty, prejudice, verbal/emotional abuse, and intolerance. "Projections," according to Jung, "change the world into the replica of one's own unknown face" (ibid., p. 96). Jung used to say that we should be grateful to those whom we make our enemies, for their darkness allows us to escape our own (Johnson 1993, p. 15). In other words, Hildegard's thirty-five vices run riot. Dishonoring our shadow by refusing to deal with its presence within our personality also results in acedia, depression, ennui, inner emptiness, and inability to establish mutuality in relationships, self-absorption, and psychosomatic illnesses. When we refuse accountability for the darker, even demonic, realities within our personalities, we project them onto others or internalize them as pathological physical or emotional symptoms. When we bury our human potential for both good and evil, we create pathology. We suffer the loss of the facility for authentically honest self-reflection, which is an increasingly important human faculty in times such as ours.

To confront a person with his shadow is to show him his own light. . . . Anyone who perceives his shadow and his light simultaneously sees himself from two sides and thus gets in the middle.

—C. G. Jung, "Good and Evil in Analytical Psychology," par. 872

To be confronted with the shadow is to be shown the light. . . . One who perceives the shadow and light simultaneously sees oneself from two sides and thus gets in the middle.

—an inclusive version of Jung on the shadow

Authentic wholeness, holiness, health, and healing for Hildegard and Jung were essentially related to the awakening to the deeper realms of inner consciousness. Hildegard's bold acknowledgment in word, music, and image of the dynamic engagement with the dark side of the soul intrigued Jung and led him to see her as an important warrant for his own thinking on the necessity of the encounter with the unconscious:

> I myself know a few individuals who have had personal experience of this phenomenon. . . . which, as Hildegard implies, brings into awareness areas of psychic happenings ordinarily covered in darkness. . . . Its effect is astonishing in that it almost always brings about a solution of psychic complications and frees the inner personality from emotional and intellectual entanglements, thus creating a unity of being which is universally felt as "liberation." (1957, par. 43)

We return to the beginning of this chapter, by recognizing how close this Jungian insight is to the spiritual vision that underlies the principles of recovery found in the program of Alcoholics Anonymous. Following a plan for spiritual progress is the way to inner harmony, well being, and serenity discovered through the fearless and thorough coming to terms with the spirits in their extraordinary variety of light and dark, creativity and destructiveness.

Every Alcoholics Anonymous meeting opens with someone reading "How It Works," which goes in part:

> Rarely have we seen a person fail who has thoroughly followed our path. Those who do not recover are people who cannot or will not completely give themselves to this simple program, usually men and women who are constitutionally incapable of being honest with themselves. There are such unfortunates. They are not at fault; they seem to have been born that way. They are naturally incapable of grasping and developing a manner of living which demands rigorous honesty. Their chances are less than average. There are those, too, who suffer from grave emotional and mental disorders, but many of them do recover if they have the capacity to be honest . . .

> With all earnestness at our command, we beg of you to be
> fearless and thorough from the very start. Some of us have tried
> to hold on to our old ideas and the result was nil until we let go
> absolutely.
>
> Remember that we deal with alcohol—cunning, baffling,
> powerful! Without help it is too much for us. But there is One
> who has all power—that One is God. May you find him now.[4]

Jung noted that Hildegard's courageous engagement with the dark
spirits brought about a solution to psychic complications and their
emotional and intellectual entanglements, which resulted in a unity
of being experienced as liberation. The essence of Hildegardian
insight is that physical problems are a sign of deeper imbalances
within the soul and the path to restoration of well being is found
through encounter with the forces of darkness. This liberation is
the hard-won work of honest self-examination that includes, in
Jung's view, the making of an inventory of psychic contents that
includes shadow material. This is a primary step in the process
toward wholeness and healing. Once the shadow is acknowledged
and felt as an *inner fact* of one's own personality, there is less chance
of projection and greater likelihood that perception and judgment
in thinking and acting will be creative and not destructive (Stein,
ed., 1996, p. 11). Thus, the simple wisdom of the twelve steps
identifies a path toward healing the rifts that fracture the human
spirit, including these steps:

4. Made a searching and fearless moral inventory
   of ourselves.

5. Admitted to God, to ourselves, and to another
   human being the exact nature of our wrongs.

6. Were entirely ready to have God remove all
   these defects of character.

I'm not sure that our embedded defects of character actually
leave the aura of our personality, but I am convinced that awareness
of them, claiming them as belonging to oneself, and working
consciously with them results in an overall healthier and serene

inner life and world of relationships. In a sense, we truly accept the reality that, while being good, we are not as good as we think we are!

Both Hildegard and Jung believed that we must befriend these shadow elements of who we are, tame them, and ultimately integrate them into ourselves so that they have limited destructive play in our daily lives. In turn, as more and more people take seriously the responsibility for their own consciousness, it will create an aggregate of collective energy sufficient to turn the tides and lead us not into temptation but deliver us from evil. We shall spend our lives wondering and often worrying about the finality of our fragile, fallen, and wondrous individual lives and the fate of our war-wearied earth. So much lies beyond the scope of our limited comprehension and imagination. Yet, as Stein so aptly says, "the best we can do is to participate in this unfolding with the greatest possible extent of consciousness. Beyond that we must reconcile ourselves to leaving the outcome up to the Power that is greater than ourselves" (Stein, ed., 1996, p. 21).

Notes

1. The *Book of Divine Works* (*De operatione Dei*) was composed between 1163–1173 CE. The mid-nineteenth-century French scholar-priest Jacques Paul Migne completed the first modern edition of Hildegard of Bingen's texts. He states that the complete title of this work is "The Book of Divine Works as Written Down by a Simple Human Being." The illuminations that accompany the text are described by Hildegard but not executed by her hand. They were painted some twenty-one years after her death.

2. Recently, Kathleen Norris, in *Acedia and Me: A Marriage, Monks, and a Writer's Life* (2008), resurrected a soul-crippling spiritual vice known as "acedia," which monks and nuns have suffered for millennia. Norris comprehensively explores aspects of the same spiritual malady identified by Hildegard.

3. For detailed treatment of Jung's thinking on the integration of evil into nature of God, see Jung's "Answer to Job" (1952), Stein's *Jung on Evil* (ed., 1996), and *In God's Shadow: The Collaboration of Victor White and C. G. Jung* by Ann Conrad Lammers (1994).

4. The complete text for "How It Works," from *The Big Book* of Alcoholics Anonymous, pp. 58–60:

Rarely have we seen a person fail who has thoroughly followed our path. Those who do not recover are people who cannot or will not completely give themselves to this simple program, usually men and women who are constitutionally incapable of being honest with themselves. There are such unfortunates. They are not at fault; they seem to have been born that way. They are naturally incapable of grasping and developing a manner of living which demands rigorous honesty. Their chances are less than average. There are those, too, who suffer from grave emotional and mental disorders, but many of them do recover if they have the capacity to be honest.

Our stories disclose in a general way what we used to be like, what happened, and what we are like now. If you have decided that you want what we have and are willing to go to any length to get it—then you are ready to take certain steps.

At some of these we balked. We thought that we could find an easier, softer way. But we could not. With all earnestness at our command, we beg of you to be fearless and thorough from the very start. Some of us have tried to hold on to our old ideas and the result was nil until we let go absolutely.

Remember that we deal with alcohol—cunning, baffling, powerful! Without help it is too much for us. But there is One who has all power—that One is God. May you find him now.

Half measures availed us nothing. We stood at the turning point. We asked His protection and care with complete abandon.

Here are the steps we took, which are suggested as a program of recovery:

1. We admitted we were powerless over alcohol—that our lives had become unmanageable.

2. Came to believe that a Power greater than ourselves could restore us to sanity.

3. Made a decision to turn our will and our lives over to the care of God as we understood Him.

4. Made a searching and fearless moral inventory of ourselves.

5. Admitted to God, to ourselves, and to another human being the exact nature of our wrongs.

6. Were entirely ready to have God remove all these defects of character.

7. Humbly asked Him to remove our shortcomings.

8. Made a list of all persons we had harmed, and became willing to make amends to them all.

9. Made direct amends to such people wherever possible, except when to do so would injure them or others.

10. Continued to take personal inventory and when we were wrong promptly admitted it.

11. Sought through prayer and meditation to improve our conscious contact with God as we understood Him, praying only for knowledge of His will for us and the power to carry that out.

12. Having had a spiritual awakening as a result of these steps, we tried to carry this message to alcoholics, and to practice these principles in all our affairs.

Many of us exclaimed, "What an order! I can't go through with it." Do not be discouraged. No one among us has been able to maintain anything like perfect adherence to these principles. We are not saints. The point is, that we were willing to grow along spiritual lines. The principles we have set down are guides to progress. We claim spiritual progress rather than spiritual perfection.

Our description of the alcoholic, the chapter of the agnostic, and our personal adventures before and after make clear three pertinent ideas:

(a) That we were alcoholic and could not manage our own lives.

(b) That probably no human power could have relieved our alcoholism.

(c) That God could and would if He were sought.

Application

Take a few moments and re-read "How It Works" from pages 100–101.

Spend some time journaling about your experience of self-honesty: of your own and of what you have observed in others.

Experiment with step 4 by making a searching and fearless moral inventory. Consider the act of writing honestly and courageously your list of shortcomings *and* virtues.

Honestly and courageously spend time journaling about your experience of wrongdoing—intended and unintended hurtful outcomes of your attitudes and actions.

Next, if you wish to explore step 5, admit to God, to yourself, and to another human being the exact nature of your wrongs. If you wish, share with a trusted other.

Finally, spend time with what you wrote about this meditation-in-action and conclude the process (this may have taken days, weeks, or months to complete) by recording what it was like to be this self-aware and transparent.

CHAPTER 5

Hildegard's Feminine Divine

Who shall find a valiant woman?

—Proverbs 31

God acts in a manly fashion when he infuses in us
the strength to be just and
not to give way before injustice;
God acts like a woman when he arouses
in us penance and shows his mercy.

—Hildegard of Bingen, *Book of Divine Works*

How could the Mother ordained from of old,
from eternity, not preexist with her Son
in a mysterious unity?

—Anonymous, *Speculum virginum (Mirror of Virgins)*, ca. 1140

The Incarnation is the descent of spirit-man,
thereby spiritualizing matter, earth, woman.
The Assumption is the ascent of woman, earth, matter,
thereby materializing heaven.

—Vera Von Der Heydt, *Prospects for the Soul*

Hildegard's Caritas is God's love for the world
as well as the world's love for God.
She is the love that beckons us to wonder but also
the love that summons us to work.

—Barbara Newman, *Sister Wisdom*

Hildegard was the first medieval woman to reflect and write at length on women. Her theological writings, poetry, sung chant, and artistic illuminations are filled with an array of feminine figures and images. The intellectual inheritance of medieval thinkers came from biblical and philosophical sources in which women's inherent inferiority was taken for granted. This is the tradition in which Hildegard was shaped and one which she accepted as the natural. Within the social and religious structures of Hildegard's time, everyone knew his or her place as having been preordained by God (Craine 1997, p. 23). Inherent female weakness required inherent masculine strength to maintain God's given order. As noted, she repeatedly minimized herself, yet was in fact an inexhaustible individual of great erudition. By inverting gender roles, Hildegard presented women as virile, strong, and virtuous and men as lax and weak. This, of course, would give credence to her authority to speak out against the Crusades and the mounting internal corruption of the ordained church leaders precisely because the source of her authority was God working through her feminine frailty to challenge "womanish" clerics, secular leaders, and ecclesiastical hierarchy. Hildegard was a confounding counterpoint to the prevailing images of women as seducers and temptresses.

Hildegard was a master at gender inversion—the literary device used to capture the attention of wayward clerics and shame them through her "virility" and "potency" with God's burning message. All the while, Hildegard was essentially theologically, ecclesially, and socially orthodox. As medieval historian and Hildegard scholar Barbara Newman notes: "Hildegard did not call for radical change of the social or ecclesiastical structures; it was the abuse of authority, not the nature of it, she opposed" (*Scivias* 1990, p. 20). That being the undisputed case, Hildegard was, however, decidedly pro-female.

While Hildegard did not question the power arrangements of patriarchy, she was, as previously discussed, surprisingly anti-dualistic in her thinking. In finding conflicts or tensions in Hildegard's thinking, one must be careful not to project a contemporary feminist hermeneutic on Hildegard's work. Within the context of her German tradition, Hildegard is clearly more conservative than what one finds in much of the literature since the 1980s arising from a North American context (for a discussion of this point, see Russell 1989). While not critiquing the misogyny of systemic patriarchy, Hildegard's visions, theology, and scientific commentaries celebrated the positive in female being and physicality. Hildegard did this without a substantial concern regarding the subordinate position of women in society or church because she did not perceive these arrangements to be in conflict with God's intention in creation. Hildegard was once challenged by another Rhineland *magistra*, Tengswindis, about her rule to admit only women of nobility bringing with them substantive endowments to her community: "Still, we know you are doing this on some reasonable ground, not unaware that in the earliest Church the Lord chose fishermen, the lowly and the poor" (Dronke 1984, p. 165). At the same time, Hildegard's novelty of thought and imaginative inventiveness makes her one of the major creative figures of the twelfth century precisely because she was able to transcend conventional expectations imposed by centuries of female subordination and the churchmen of her own era (Constant Mews, quoted in D'Arcens and Ruys 2004, p. 90).

Her theology and science are rich in positive references to gestation, motherhood, the womb, sexuality, and *viriditas,* which she saw as the feminine life principle of moist greenness, fertility, and lushness. In Hildegard's visions, the Godhead is depicted symbolically, often by the mere presence of the color gold or as a feminine figure and, at other times, a bearded masculine figure. Her use of color and gender balance opens the image of God and God's nature to a theologically and symbolically rich multidimensionalism. The positive feminine in Hildegard's visions and her commitment to the manifestation of what has come to be called "the feminine divine" provide an interesting window into some of the ways she foreshadowed the important role that the feminine plays in Jungian depth psychology. This chapter explores Hildegard's pro-female orientation to Christian theology and spirituality and how it intersected with Jung's own work on retrieving the balance of feminine and masculine in the Trinitarian life of God.

Christ's Humanity

Hildegard was the first who saw woman as the symbol of normative humanity. This may not seem like a revolutionary statement on a page in a book published in the twenty-first century when it has for some time been unacceptable to subsume the female in the male pronoun or comfortably permit the use of mankind as a linguistic symbol for all of humanity. But for Hildegard in her time to suggest that woman is an autonomous fitting image for humanity is no less than a revolution of thinking and theology. For Hildegard, Christ's humanity was to his divinity as woman is to man. In the *Book of Divine Works,* Hildegard states: "Man signifies the divinity of the son of God and woman his humanity." In a surprising shift in theological anthropology, woman is the representative human being. The Woman, meaning Mary's singular feat of elevating all women's flesh, shared the vessel-capacity of the Incarnation, the clothing of Christ's own physicality. Mary confected the body of Christ within her physicality and by doing so elevated the status of female nature to something more than the dominant culture allowed. Mary's singularity does not separate her from other women but confers distinction upon all women. Related to her vision in *Scivias* I.4 (see plate 8), Hildegard, in the *Book of Divine Works,* went on to say:

> Now when God looked upon man he was well pleased, for he had created him after the tunic of his image and after his likeness, to proclaim all these marvels through the trumpet of a rational voice. For man is the consummate work of God. It is he who knows God, and for his sake created all creatures, and, in the kiss of true love, enabled him to proclaim and praise through his reason. (Newman 1987, p. 94)

With sharp insight, Barbara Newman offers an exegesis of the symbolic meaning of the words *tunic* and *trumpet*. She suggests that the trumpet image is to be understood as the capacity for intelligent communication and it resides in the soul; the tunic refers to bodily form. Hildegard said that the "tunic of Christ's humanity" was assumed from woman (Newman 1987, p. 94).[1] Newman goes on to say:

Herein lies the clue to Hildegard's surprisingly radical anthropology, which would exalt not the male but the female as the representative human being . . . It is not by her appearance but by her gift that the woman represents Christ's human nature and bears the stamp of his image . . . so at every level the feminine is that in God which binds itself most intimately with the human race, and through it with the cosmos. Conversely, the feminine aspect of humanity is that which enters into union with God: Mary, the Church, the Virtues, the virginal soul, and even the humanity of Christ are now seen as female. (Ibid., pp. 93, 250)

We may never be able to determine with precision
how forms acquired through learning were
recombined in Hildegard's mind to create new images . . .
Whether we treat them as explosions from the unconscious
or as meticulously cultivated growths.

—Kent Kraft, *Medieval Women Writers*

Human nature belongs to the woman as gift. Her reciprocity, symbolized in Mary and the Incarnation, transformed a purely pejorative dualistic vision of the female body—pure matter (*mater,* "mother" in Latin, from the *materia*), sensual, material, of the created world and its attendant evil—to be a place of God's inception as divine incarnation. Hildegard gave a twist, an extraordinary twist, to theological anthropology by granting representative humanity to the female. Hildegard's "divinely inspired" positive regard for femaleness offers an unexpected, even if unwanted, correction to the prevailing thinking of her time. Hildegard accepted female weakness and frailty as in need of masculine strength and intellect, and at the same time, announced female nature in all its bodiliness to be the place of divine animation and self-disclosure. It seems clear that Hildegard had an intention, through the inspiration of the Holy Spirit, to correct the exclusion of the feminine from the life of the Trinity. For Jung, Hildegard provided a theologically satisfying solution to the psychological problem posed by Western Christianity's Trinitarian doctrine of God.

The Vision of the Soul's Journey

Jung titles section V in *Civilization in Transition* "Flying Saucers: A Modern Myth of Things Seen in the Skies." In this section, he explores unidentified flying objects (UFOs) as consequential psychologically with respect to their meanings arising from the unconscious. His purpose is to treat UFOs as a psychological phenomenon. He asks, "What is the meaning of such a rumour at the present time? What future developments are being prepared in the unconscious of modern man?" (1958, par. 731). Jung is exploring artists' renderings rich with symbols suggesting that UFOs are subliminal contents that are becoming visible; that they are, in a word, archetypal figures (ibid., par. 747). In a somewhat offbeat way, Jung discusses, while offering an interpretation of the UFO phenomenon, a synchronicity with Hildegard's illumination discussed above that also treats quaternity in the Trinity: the feminine dimension which adds a fourth to the Trinitarian three in order to create true unity in God. Before exploring Jung's reference to Hildegard's "remarkable symbolism" in the illumination from the *Scivias*, a further explanation is in order. The vision from the *Scivias* depicts the soul's journey. It is described by many titles, including "God is present when a child is born/stages of life under God's tent" and "Body and Soul," and Jung identifies it as "The Quickening of the Child in the Womb." This rich image provides an apt example of how Hildegard thought it better to work with symbols than the naked word. This is yet another reason why Hildegard appealed to Jung. He longed for all Christian doctrine to be recast in symbolic mode so that theology would enjoy a thorough appreciation of how symbol functioned in the human psyche. Hildegard was evidently naturally inclined in that direction. It is obvious from the complexity of her visions and commentary associated with each image that it is not always clear or easy to grasp the fullness of her theological and spiritual treatments of various themes.

In this instance, Hildegard sees a golden kite-shaped figure, in flames, with many open eyes illuminating the star-filled sky. Its flaming brilliance signifies the Mystery of God's eternal counsel, which extends its gaze to the four corners of the earth—north, south, east, and west—and clearly sees all good and evil. From the center of the Godhead—the Mystery of the Trinity—a golden cord flows into the egg-shaped image below it. Like an umbilical cord, it connects God's transcendence to the womb of the woman pregnant with child. In this marvelous vision of the four-sided Trinity—representing the four corners of the world—the golden umbilical cord reaches into the womb of the Woman (prototype of Mary) to vivify the baby resting, clothed with and in the Woman's womb. A womb clothes divinity. There is maternity in the Trinity. As Divine Personhood enters the soul at birth, it enters the body, too. Mary's (the Woman's) physical motherhood is the instrument of the delivery of Christ into his humanity, which in turn, becomes the medium of his divinity. Divinity is aimed at humanity; humanity connected to Divinity. The Divine Motherhood, Womb of the Word made flesh, is no less consequential than the Divine Fatherhood of God (Sur 1993, p.138). Father and mother are reunited.

The panels on the side are read from the bottom up and touch upon the struggle of the soul to "set up its tent," meaning, biblically speaking, the journey of the soul seeking to dwell in peace with Holy Presence. Along with maternity in divinity, the illumination includes the soul's engagement with the forces of evil inherent in the journey to wholeness. As Jung notes, "The devil, too, has a hand in the game" (1958, par. 769). This is a significant intersection for Hildegard and Jung. The values of consciousness in the spiritual patriarchal worldview include Father-God, Spirit (reason), and Christ. Excluded are femaleness, body, and Satan. In Hildegard's quaternity, the spirit moves to the unity of male/female, body/spirit, and Christ (good)/Satan (evil). Interestingly, Hildegard's illumination symbolically illustrates important aspects of Jung's vision of psychological wholeness. Here Hildegard gives witness to her critique of dualism that insisted on an eternal chasm between divinity and humanity, as well as offers a theological anthropology that is decidedly pro-female. As Carolyn Sur notes:

> In medieval numerology a special significance is given to the number four. In the interpretations of number symbolism, four, not three, represents completeness. Without the fourth dimension, the Trinity, in medieval numerology, is incomplete.

Thus, the significance of the reality in this work is, that without the feminine dimension in the Godhead—the dimension that motherhood brings—the Trinity, in this sense, is an incomplete representation of humanity created male and female in the image of God. (1993, p. 154)

Mary and the Trinity

Jung was clearly intrigued by how illustrative this medieval vision was in providing him another avenue of retrieval of the fourness important to a psychological vision based on completeness and the restoration of the feminine dimension to the Godhead. Jung's effort to "treat" the maladies besetting Christianity included seeking its redemption from the partialness that he saw exemplified in the suppression of the feminine and stubborn fixation on a dualistic worldview. Again, it is important to note that Jung sometimes blurred the lines between doctrinal theology and therapy, acting as theologian more than psychologist. In doing so, he was specifically seeking a therapeutic design for a Christianity whose practical life could produce healing in fractured human souls.[2] Jung saw the normative doctrine of the Trinity as having a central error: a procession of masculine Gods-in-One, from which the feminine element is missing. Theologian Mary Daly expressed it this way:

[Christianity's] symbol of processions is the all-male trinity itself. Of obvious significance here is the fact that this is an image of the procession of the divine son from the divine father (no mother or daughter involved). In this symbol the first person, the father, is the origin who thinks forth the second person, the son, the word, who is the perfect image of himself, who is "co-eternal" and "consubstantial," that is identical in essence. So total is their union that their "mutual love" is expressed by the procession (known as "spiration") of a third person called the "Holy Spirit," whose proper name is Love. This naming of "the three Divine Persons" is the paradigmatic model for the pseudogeneric term *person*, excluding all female mythic presence, denying female reality in the cosmos. (1978, pp. 37–38)[3]

By correcting the missing fourth from the "procession" of divine becoming, a new symbolic shift takes place that recognizes the completion of the Three in Four. This new symbolic shift works to heal the rift between spirit and matter that would help with the evolution of Christianity (Stein 1985, p. 158).

In the history of symbols,
quaternity is the unfolding of unity.

—C. G. Jung, *Civilization in Transition,* par. 774

It is not surprising that Jung found Pope Pius XII's pronouncement in 1950 of the Dogma of the Assumption of Mary to be a "radical new step toward integrating the repressed" (Stein 1985, p. 124). He referred to it as "the most important religious event since the Reformation" (1952, par. 752). Through this dogma of faith, the feminine is recalled to the realm of the divine. The Church proclaimed "that the Immaculate Mother of God, the ever Virgin Mary, having completed the course of her earthly life, was assumed body and soul into heavenly glory." The emphasis is on Mary's humanity, that is, on her womanhood and on her body. The dogma asserts: "We hope that the exalted destiny of both our soul and body may in this striking manner be brought to notice by all [people]." The promulgation of this dogma followed centuries of preparation in the collective unconscious, as evidenced by the many apparitions of Mary, such as Fatima and Lourdes, and by the popular religiosity nourished through Marian piety and rituals of devotion. Mary has been important in Christian theology and the practice of the faith not only as a historical figure. Her life is regarded symbolically as a pattern for behavior and a model of possibilities for transformation that all persons carry within themselves (Von Der Heydt 1976, p. 71). According to Von Der Heydt in an engaging chapter called "Psychological Implications of the Dogma of the Assumption," Eve is symbolic of the human attempt towards greater consciousness and the search for the ego, whereas Mary represents the birth of the Self. In this regard, Eve and Mary are our two mothers: each other's opposite side. Together they generate the archetype of the *Magna Mater*, the sacred earth mother of us all (ibid., p. 72). Stein suggests that by including the *body* of the Virgin, Christianity was expanding away from a purely spiritual (masculine) conception of God toward a symbolic image that would include human flesh and its vulnerabilities within the doctrine of God (1985, pp. 124, 169). This again is a depth psychological rendering; theologically speaking, such was not intended by Rome. That Hildegard could paint the Trinity as four-sided is truly amazing, and Jung took notice. Normative Christianity, however, is still at some distance from such an understanding of Trinitarian life.

She is not only the feminine principle,
but the actual woman who carries the
darkness of woman in her blood.
By her reactions to the situations confronting her,
she transforms the archetypal dark desire "to be like God"
into acceptance and realization of her body as channel
through which spirit is born into the world.
Thereby she changes Eve's name; *mutans nomen
Evae—Eva-Ave*, as she is greeted by the angel Gabriel.

—Vera Von Der Heydt, *Prospects for the Soul*

In Her We See Who We Can Be

In 1854, nearly a century before the Dogma of the Assumption, Pope Pius IX promulgated the Dogma of the Immaculate Conception. This dogma declared that "the most Blessed Virgin Mary was, from the first moment of her conception, by a singular grace and privilege of almighty God and by virtue of the merits of Jesus Christ, Savior of the human race, preserved immune from all stain of original sin." While nearly a century of development brought Marian theology to the declaration of the Assumption, it is an assumption of a *sinless* body; nonetheless, it is a *female body* of the one named

Theotokos: God-bearer. Again, Catholic theology was not altered in the ways Jung hoped; nonetheless, Newman says that Jung "had put his finger on an aspect of Catholic art and devotion that has yet to be fully explored by historians of spirituality" (Newman 2003, p. 255). The Divine "decends" in the Incarnation, re-sacralizing creation, earth, woman; the Assumption is the "ascent" of woman, flesh, earth, matter, thereby "materializing" heaven (Von Der Heydt 1976, p. 76). Mary achieves an at-one-ment of matter and spirit, which becomes a developmental task for all—in her, we see who we can be. I would add that Catholic theology has yet to fully explore the value of Jung's insights into a contemporary reinterpretation of these aspects of Mariology. Jungian David Richo, in *Mary Within Us* (2007), provides fresh and engaging insights that prompt dialogue about Mary as a personification of the virtues and the destiny of the human psyche, including the often unexplored dark side.

Jung devotes three pages in *Civilization in Transition* to discussing the remarkable symbolism of "The Quickening of the Child in the Womb." Jung focuses on Hildegard's explication of "countless eyes" and the transcultural notion of the divine eye motif. In addition, Jung explores at some length the meaning of "the squareness of the Holy Ghost." He says,

> The square, being a quaternity, is a totality symbol in alchemy. Having four corners it signifies the earth, whereas a circular form is attributed to the spirit. Earth is feminine, spirit masculine. The square as a symbol of the spiritual world is certainly most unusual, but becomes more intelligible when we take Hildegard's sex into account. This remarkable symbolism is reflected in the squaring of the circle—another *coniunctio oppositorum* [conjunction/reconciliation of opposites]. (1958, par. 767)

[I]f the individuation process is made conscious,
consciousness must confront the unconscious
and a balance between the opposites must be found.
As this is not possible through logic,
one is dependent on *symbols*
which make the irrational union of opposites possible.

—C. G. Jung, *Answer to Job*, par. 755

PLATE I

"Hildegard of Bingen," copyright 2002 by Cynthia Large.
Used with permission of the artist.

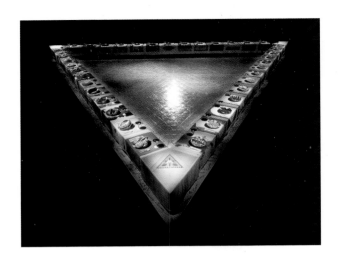

PLATES 2 & 3

The Dinner Party is on permanent display at the Brooklyn Museum in
The Elizabeth A. Sackler Center for Feminist Art. See the online virtual
tour at www.brooklynmuseum.org. © 1979, Judy Chicago. The Dinner
Party. Placesetting for Hildegarde of Bingen Collection Brooklyn
Museum, Gift of the Elizabeth A. Sackler Foundation.
Photos © Donald Woodman.

PLATE 4
Iceberg © Ralph A. Clevenger/CORBIS.
Used with permission.

ad exponendum·⁊ indocta ad scriben
dum ea dic ⁊ scribe illa ñ scdm os̄ homi
nis·nec scdm intellectum humanę ad
inuentionis nec scdm uoluntatē huma
nę compositionis s̄ scdm id quod ea in
celestib̄ desup in mirabilib̄ dī uides ⁊ au
dis·ea sic edisserendo pferens·quemadmo
dum ⁊ auditor uerba p̄ceptoris sui p̄cipi
ens·ea scdm tenorē locutionis illi·ipso uo
lente·ostendente·⁊ p̄cipiente ppalat·Sic
⁊ ⁊ tu ó homo·dic ea q̄ uides ⁊ audis·⁊ sc̄
be ea non scdm te·nec scdm aliū homi
nem·s̄ secundū uoluntatē scientis uiden
tis·⁊ disponentis omnia in secretis miste
rioru̅ suoru̅·Et iteru̅ audiui uoce̅
de celo michi dicente·Dic ⁊ mirabilia
hec·⁊ scribe ea hoc modo edocta ⁊ dic·

Factum e̅ in millesimo centesimo
quadragesimo p̄mo filii dī ihū xp̄
incarnationis anno·cū q̄draginta duoꝛ
annoꝛ septe q; insum eēm maxime consca
tionis igneū lumē apto celo ueniens totū
cerebrū meū trisfudit·⁊ totū cor totu̅q;
pectus meū uelut flamma ñ tam ar
dens s̄ calens ita inflammauit·ut sol
rem aliquam calefacit·sup quam radi
os suos ponit·Et repente intellectum
expositionis libroꝛ uidelicet·psalterii
euuangelii ⁊ alioꝛ catholicoꝛ tam ue
teris quam noui testamenti uolumi
num sapiebam·ñ aute̅ inp̄retatio
nem uerboꝛ textus eoꝛ nec diuisione̅

Et ecce quadra
gesimo tercio
temporalis cur
sus mei anno
cum celesti uisi
oni magno ti
more ⁊ tremu
la intentione inhererem uidi maxi
mū splendorē·in quo facta e̅ uox
de celo ad me dicens·O homo fragi
lis ⁊ cinis cineris ⁊ putredo putredi
nis·dic ⁊ scribe q̄ uides ⁊ audis·Sed
quia timida es ad loquendū ⁊ simplex

PLATES **6** & **7**

The four seasons and man as the center of
the universe, from "De Operatione Dei."
Photo credit: Scala / Art Resource, NY.

PLATE 8

From *Scivias* (Know the ways of the Lord)
by Hildegard von Bingen. *left*: God is present when
a child is born. *right*: Stages of life under God's tent.
Photo credit: Erich Lessing /Art Resource, NY.

PLATE **9**

Hildegard in Episcopal vestments.
Photo credit : Erich Lessing / Art Resource, NY.

The notion of the transformational integration of the opposites is important here because Jung sees Hildegard's vision and her reinterpretation of Christian doctrine as central to the kind of new Christianity he perceived as necessary for the vitality of the tradition and its evolution to meet the needs of modern consciousness. Mary, and through her all women, and the feminine principle is introduced into the Trinitarian life of God and thus represents a transformation of tremendous import. The hostile *oppositorum* between masculine/feminine, soul/body, and spirit/matter find *coniunctio* in the doctrine proposed by Hildegard and reinforced, at least for Jung, in the Dogma of Mary's Assumption.

> In Hildegard's songs to Mary,
> she is the "greenest twig"; not
> even a branch, a twig. Yet,
> she is green with God's pregnant
> vitality, and her comparative insignificance
> (as a woman, and unmarried)
> prepares her for the greatness of God's Spirit
> to grow within her and produce the miraculous
> "flowering" of God's divine-human Son.
> Her weakness is her strength.
>
> —Carmen Acevedo Butcher, "Hildegard of Bingen
>   and Her Love of the Polysemous Logos"

Conclusion

Hildegard gave a new appreciation for feminine weakness that both accepted the positive in the female and used it to criticize her "effeminate age" in which men had grown "womanish." Her visions revealed rich theology and great artistry with central figures that were often depicted in female form: Ekklesia, Caritas, Scientia Dei, the Virtues, Pure Knowledge.[4] In short, Newman summarized:

> To see the feminine as a species of incapacity and frailty,
> yet also as a numinous and salvific dimension of the divine

nature: herein lies the characteristic strain of what I have called
Hildegard's "theology of the feminine." (1987, pp. 35–36)

We may boldly claim Hildegard as the first Christian thinker
to deal seriously and positively with the feminine as such, not
merely with the challenges posed by and for women in a male-
dominated world. (Ibid., p. xvii)

In sum, we have in Hildegard von Bingen a woman whose chronic
illnesses and inner visions were both a burden and a gift. In her
feminine frailty, she permitted the strength of God's message to be
heard by one small trumpet. And through all this she was very much a
Benedictine nun steeped within monastic and patriarchal traditions.
The rise of feminine imagery in her time afforded her the opportunity
to explore the contours of her and other women's religious experience
and to permit the female person and the feminine in the Godhead to
be celebrated in prose, poetry, and music. While she did this without
critique concerning the structures of female subordination in culture
and religion, she nonetheless left an unparalleled prophetic and
intellectual legacy ripe for future generations to develop. Jung was
one such developer that found in her something of value to his own
important transformational work.

There is in Hildegard a curious tension that, coupled with Jung's
insistence on quest for the integration of the masculine and feminine
energies, presents the contemporary spiritual seeker with a paradox.
One way to characterize this paradox is to say that Hildegard
appeared to be in complicity with the gender expectations of her
times, while her lived witness to female potency and potentiality
suggest a fuller story. On the one hand, she accepted the traditional
view of the female as passive. On the other hand, she did not see
this passivity as merely a negative property—as solely pejorative
weakness. She saw female weakness as itself a kind of potency—a
specifically female kind, namely, fecundity, *viriditas*. She grounded
the validity of her inner experience within the theological tradition
of Mary and proceeded to become a theological innovator whose
insights, like Jung's, we are still mining for deeper meaning. She
emphasized "female" reproductive powers in such a way that they
became, in their way, as potent as "male" productive powers. Hence,
she could be "God's trumpet": her "trumpeting" was not "male"

assertiveness but "female" receptivity to the Holy Spirit—assisting the Divine Desire to incarnate into a wholeness and reconciliation of opposites.

And finally, perhaps there is something else here, something implicit in her self-portrayal as a "poor little figure" at a time of crisis in the church. Perhaps, in Hildegard, we have a model of challenge for contemporary women who struggle with the paradox of female and feminine gender expectations and the call of duty and daring required in an ongoing turbulent time of transition.

In light of Hildegard's brilliant theology, her holistic worldview, and her positive appropriation of the feminine and female nature relative to the Divine, I am led to wonder if the leap from being *in persona Spiritus Dei* is not so far from standing *in persona Christi?* *In persona Christi* means taking on the role of Christ to the point of being his very image. Simply put, Hildegard's theological anthropology does allow for the ontological warrant for the female to be *in persona Christi* even if her ecclesiology does not. This raises the provocative and vexing question of gender, female religious leadership, and duty and daring in the life of the church today.

Notes

1. At the same time, it ought not to be lost that Hildegard also referred to herself as "a small trumpet of the Living Light." In helping other female mystics struggling with their interior life, Hildegard suggested that they follow her in being "like a trumpet which resounds not by its own effort but by the breath of another." This, of course, was in reference to Hildegard's famous depiction of herself in relation to the Living Light within: "I am but a feather on the breath of God."

2. For Jung's discussion of the Christian Trinity, see *Psychology and Religion;* for a comprehensive explanation of Jung's therapeutic vision of subjecting Christianity to psychological analysis, see Stein 1985.

3. Ideas in quotes refer to Thomas Aquinas, *Summa theologiae* I, q. 37. It would be a disservice to Daly to rely on her metaphysical and theological summation of Trinitarian life without noting that, in this same text, she rails against female Jungians by saying, "Particularly seductive is the illusion of equality projected through Jung's androcratic animus-anima balancing act, since women are trained to be grateful for 'complementarity' and token inclusion. Tokenism is embedded in the very fabric of Jung's ideology . . . ."

Thus it is possible for women to promote Jung's garbled gospel without awareness of betraying their own sex, and even in the belief that they are furthering the feminist cause" (1978, p. 280).

4. On the virtues as feminine in nature, Hildegard's *Book of Divine Works* notes: "In the fullness of time God became a human being: The Word came to pass in the cosmos; Christ reveals himself in three basic virtues: Love [*Caritas*], Humility [*Humilitas*], and Peace [*Pax*]."

Application

Sandra Schneiders addresses the problem of God language in the article "God is More Than Two Men and a Bird." She says:

> God is spirit, neither male nor female. All our language of God is metaphorical. Metaphors are tensive images. That means that they are simultaneously to be upheld and negated. God is our father and God is not our father; God is our mother and not our mother. If we forget the "is not," then we create an idol—that is, we make God into the image of a creature. By keeping our metaphors of God active simultaneously, we keep ourselves aware that none of them is to be taken literally and that none of them is adequate for the Holy Mystery who is God. (1990, pp. 20–22)

> How has your image of God changed over the years? Is there a new God-image incubating within your spiritual life and imagination today? What images are awakening in you?

Hildegard and Jung both explored new visions of Christianity while they experienced living in transitional times. All transitional periods include the experience of doubt, chaos, and disorientation. The contemporary woman and man are now living in a turbulent era of transition with its consequent rise of creativity and equally strong demonic manifestations.

A key step in the direction of individuation is to take back projections of unconscious shadow by recognizing that the "enemy" is within oneself, that what one reacts to emotionally in an opponent represents an unclaimed piece of one's own psyche. Christianity has provided tremendous meaning for countless believers for millennia and, at the same time, has reinforced a split in the nature of God by insisting on the ontological superiority of maleness. Such one-sidedness in Christianity resulted in every Christian having a splintered psyche (see Daly 1978). "Naturally the lesion cannot be treated or healed if everyone insists on his own standpoint" (Stein 1985, p. 172, quoting Jung, *Mysterium conjunctionis*, p. 200).

> What is your experience of living in a time of
> transition and how do you experience resistance to and
> complicity with one-sidedness of any sort?

CHAPTER 6

Hildegard's *Mater Ecclesia* (Mother Church)

Re-vision—the act of looking back,
of seeing with fresh eyes, of entering
an old text from a critical direction—
is for women more than a chapter
in cultural history: it is an act of survival.

—Adrienne Rich, *The Dream of a Common Language*

May your leadership be a time of new growth,
not a time of shriveled expectations.

—Hildegard, letter to King Frederick

What does it mean that such secrets
are revealed by this silly,
uneducated woman when there are
so many sturdy and wise men around?

—Hildegard, in her *Vita*

The problem for women in Christian tradition
is not so much that they have been absent, as that they
have lacked legitimating power.
It's not so much that women in the Christian past have been
silent as silenced.

—Rosemary Radford Ruether, "The Task of
Feminist Theology"

I am going to do something new.
It is already happening.
Don't you recognize it?
I will clear a way in the desert.
I will make rivers on dry land.

—Isaiah 43:19

Remembering So as Not to Forget

What is the value of retrieving and reflecting upon old stories about women, like Hildegard, who lived so long ago, especially amid the urgencies that mark and mar a time such as ours? Has not the quest for a usable past—one that reincorporates women into the historical and ecclesiastical record—been an almost archeological endeavor of Christian feminism in the last decades of the twentieth century? Why keep digging? We cannot allow our zeal to flag, thinking that it has been done. Feminist recovery efforts must not be forgotten, so that new generations will not have to discover women of duty and daring all over again. So very long ago Hildegard peppered her written works and public sermons with the admonition to be wary of falling into forgetfulness. We remember so as not to forget.

This kind of remembering is not nostalgic wistfulness, melancholy or excessively sentimental yearning for a return to some distant time or irrecoverable condition. Nostalgia easily induces a state of denial evidencing a desperate attempt to cling to a past time that is no more and never will be again. Nostalgia can actually contribute to fatalistic despair, apathy (acedia), and spiritual death. I am talking about remembering as *anamnesis*: the retrieval of the deep memory that holds the transformative charism—the grace and gift yesterday, today, and forever (Hebrews 13:8). While the opposite of nostalgia is a kind of joy in the present, the antonym of *anamnesis* is amnesia: the loss of a large block of interrelated memories. It is a seriously catastrophic state to lose one's memory. Jungian depth psychology is based on the conviction that much of our emotional distress and psychic disturbance is caused by a suppression, repression, or dislocation of our current life from access to and awareness of the full memory of our past—the all of it—wonderful and wounded. The kind of remembering to which I am referring is far more than simply reclamation or revisioning of history or psychological retrieval of past times. In a sense, the past does not remain in the past, but shapes the present and the future. The poet Rilke captures the meaning of this imaginative power when he writes, in *Letters to a Young Poet* (1984, pp. 23–24):

> You must give birth to your images.
> They are the future waiting to be born.
> Fear not the strangeness you feel.
> The future must enter you
>   long before it happens,
> Just wait for the birth,
> for the hour of new clarity.

New Testament scholar Xavier Leon-Dufour argues that "memorial"—solely past-oriented—is not an adequate translation for *anamnesis*, a Greek word with deep historical roots in Jewish tradition. The problem with "memorial" is that it signifies an action already completed, rather than an action that is taking place. Eucharistic *anamnesis* is a celebration of remembrance in which the Christian community's proclamation is necessarily self-involving, transforming pastness into presence and promise, and openness to the future (Leon-Dufour 1987, p. 114). People of the Book and those who treasure the long sweep of religious history find *anamnesis* a liturgical kind of remembering. The Christian faith itself is built upon the great *anamnesis*: "Let us proclaim the mystery of faith: Christ has died, Christ is risen, Christ will come again." The lyrics to Marty Haugen's "We Remember" capture the why of the charge *to remember so as not to forget*: "We remember how you loved us to your death and still we celebrate that you are with us here; and we believe that we will see you when you come, in your glory Lord. We remember, we celebrate, we believe" (1980). This is a kind of remembering that simultaneously roots us in a permanently meaningful past, holds us meaningfully in the present, and orients us toward the future whose meaning we are called both to wait for and to bring about. Such catholic remembering effects what it signifies by evoking and provoking what Johann Baptist Metz named so long ago as dangerous memories. He defines this notion:

> There are memories in which earlier experiences break through the centre-point of our lives and reveal new and dangerous insights for our present. They illuminate for a few moments and with a harsh steady light the questionable nature of things we have apparently come to terms with, and show up the banality of our supposed "realism." They break through the canon of all that is taken as self-evident, and unmask as deception the certainty of those "whose hour is always here" (John 7:6). They seem to subvert our structures of plausibility. Such memories are like dangerous and incalculable visitants from the past. (Metz 1972, p. 15)

He goes on to say, "There are memories we have to take into account; memories, as it were, with future content" (ibid.). This chapter explores Hildegard as a visitant from the past; a dangerous memory with future content. The discussion in the following pages is "churchy," since Hildegard's life as a woman religious and ecclesial leader takes pride of place. To appreciate the prophetic in Hildegard, it is important to see her in the context of the evolution of religious leadership happening in the midst of her era. Perhaps we can see her as a model for our circumstances by seeing how she recognized yet challenged limitations, and how women in today's churches might do the same. This chapter concludes by examining Hildegard as an example of an "animus" woman, one who, in the midst of the strictures of patriarchy, found a freedom to express individuality and the process of individuation.

Pausing at Patriarchy

As discussed at the end of chapter 2, patriarchy became established as the overarching explanatory system of Western civilization, and the development of the church within this system is no exception. With that in mind, it would not be an overstatement to say that the place of women in ecclesiastical matters has vexed the Christian church for millennia. Through history and in principle the church has not recognized the female right to ecclesiastical jurisdiction except, in limited ways, in matters pertaining to female religious life. The institutional church has long mistrusted women and opposed their autonomy and decision-making. Ancient philosophy and patristic theology gradually wove the patriarchal patterns that subjugated women and eventually eroded the distinctive, egalitarian pattern of gender relations established by Jesus himself. For example, in the Letter to the Ephesians 5:22, 24, composed around 61 CE, we read: "Wives, be subjects to your husbands, as to the Lord. For the husband is the head of the wife as Christ is the head of the church . . . . as the church is subject to Christ, so let wives also be subject in everything to their husbands." By 90 CE, the following appeared in the First Letter to Timothy 2:11–12: "Let a woman learn in silence with all submissiveness. I permit no woman to teach or to have authority over men; she is to keep silent."

The system of patriarchy, whose last vestiges remain operative today, was firmly entrenched in the early medieval era. At this time, however, there was Hildegard of Bingen, an abbess who was aware of the strictures of her time but transcended them. Medievalist Caroline Walker Bynum, in *Gender and Religion*, says:

> The misogyny of the Middle Ages is well known. Not merely a defensive reaction on the part of men who were in fact social-ly, economically, and politically dominant, it was fully articu-lated in theological, philosophical, and scientific theory that was centuries old. *Male* and *female* were contrasted and asym-metrically valued as intellect/body, active/passive, rational/irra-tional, reason/emotion, self-control/lust, judgment/mercy, and order/disorder. (Bynum, Harrell, and Richman 1985, p. 257)

Interestingly, the role of the abbess during the early medieval era, to some extent, upset the patriarchal paradigm. Historian Gary Macy has powerfully argued the evidence that medieval abbesses were heirs to the ancient order of deaconess. (For a comprehensive discussion of this question, see Macy 2008.) Macy takes the position that women religious in general and abbesses in particular did not consider themselves members of the laity; they considered themselves as ordained as any male cleric of the time. Even popes of the time referred to the installation of abbesses as ordination.[1] The functioning of the abbesses eventually became increasingly vexing to canonists and popes because of the scope of their authority. Abbots and abbesses were powerful figures, often more powerful than bishops. Hildegard lived in the middle of the era that was in the process of redefining the meaning of ordination begun in the eleventh century and finally concluded by the thirteenth century.

Ultimately, the thirteenth-century redefinition of ordination narrowed to the power to consecrate the bread and wine at the altar. Sacramental mediation became the central purpose of ordination, which came to be understood metaphysically as an indelible and eternal character of the soul that bestowed power to be used by a priest in any community at any time. The preeminent Dominican philosopher-theologian Thomas Aquinas taught that a person is the union of *caro* and *anima*. Priestly ordination is bestowed upon the *anima*—to the soul—and not to the *caro*, the body. Even if, Aquinas reasoned, a woman were to receive the form of Holy Orders—be ordained to the priesthood—she would not receive the sacrament, since Holy Orders signified the eminence of degree and a female, by nature, is incapable of eminence. What this means is that a woman's innate weakness prevents the character of ordination in her soul since, by reason of sexual differentiation, the female soul is inferior in kind, deficient in spiritual receptivity and power. For Aquinas and for generations thereafter, woman is preeminently *caro* and permanently incapacitated with respect to mediating the grace of Christ in sacramental function (see McGrath 1971).

As regards the individual nature woman is defective and misbegotten, for the active force in the male seed tends to the production of a perfect likeness in the masculine sex; while the production of woman comes from defect in the active force or from some material indisposition, or even some external influence; such as that of a south wind, which is moist, as the Philosopher observes.

—Thomas Aquinas, *Summa Theologica*, 1273

The pre-thirteenth-century, older, broader definitions of ordination gradually faded away and with them went an understanding of ordination that once linked ordination to vocation, leadership, and ritual in the context of community from which the leader emerged from the community. There was no understanding during those early centuries that only priests could lead a liturgy or that only priests were ordained (Macy 2008, p. 42). This is not to say that female religious leadership thrived in a coequal untroubled environment in the early church. It is simply to note that Hildegard was shaped by a more open, albeit patriarchal, mentality concerning the *different* ways that men and women exercised ecclesial leadership. The abbess functioned like a deaconess in exercising leadership aligned with specific functions arising from a community of faith for the nurture of the spiritual life and growth of a specific community.

It was common for the abbess to be the magistrate over dual monasteries of monks and nuns. The abbatial authority of medieval nuns included the power to hold councils of other abbesses and to visit and be in dialogue with other abbeys and affiliated convents. The abbess held the spiritual power to bless, baptize, proclaim the gospel at public prayer, preach publicly, instruct, lead Eucharistic processions, distribute communion, hear the confessions of her nuns, and impose or lift excommunications. Such powers active in the twelfth century, however, would be taken away by the thirteenth century, never to be returned to the domain of female religious leadership again.

I know of two brothers who are numbered among the highest masters, the other of whom imputed such power to the divine words in the confecting of the sacrament that by whomever they are pronounced, they have the same efficacy, so that even a woman or someone of whatever order or condition through the words of the Lord is able to confect the sacrament of the altar.

—Peter Abelard (1079–1142),
Theologia Christiana (*Christian Theology*)

What kind of Christianity allowed abbesses to
hear their nuns' confessions, preach and distribute
communion? Evidence survives that describes all
of the above, and yet such evidence should not have
survived. It should never have existed at all, if the
dominant narrative were consistent.

—Gary Macy, *The Hidden History of Women's Ordination* (2008, p. 51)

Similarly, deacons must be dignified, not deceitful,
not addicted to drink, not greedy for sordid gain,
holding fast to the mystery of the faith
with a clear conscience.
Moreover, they should be tested first;
then, if there is nothing against them,
let them serve as deacons.
Women, similarly, should be dignified,
not slanderers, but temperate
and faithful in everything.

—I Timothy 3:9–11

Hildegard: A Memory with Future Content

It bears repeating that in an effort to break through the burden of
her own silence, Hildegard put her hand to writing, and proceeded
from the age of forty-three until her death at eighty-one to compose
a theological trilogy, two scientific works, the first known morality
play of the West, seventy-seven liturgical songs, and two biographical
works on the lives of St. Disibod and St. Rupert. She recorded fifty
homilies delivered on four preaching tours begun in her sixties and
maintained an active correspondence documented in more than
three hundred extant letters between herself and popes, kings,
archbishops, abbots and abbesses, other women mystics and nuns,
and lay people seeking her aid. And through all this she was very
much a Benedictine nun steeped in the traditions of her time. She

lived, wrote, and preached in the tensions between adhering to orthodoxy and the novelty of her intellectual twists and turns. Her image of herself as a "feather touched by God, suspended in the air by His breath, suggests that she speaks only through the strength and will of God and not of her own volition" (McInerney 1998, p. 15). Hildegard believed this and others believed it of her.

As explored in the previous chapter, the rise of feminine imagery in her time afforded her the opportunity to explore the contours of her and other women's religious experience and to permit the female person and the feminine in the Godhead to be celebrated in word and song. Monasticism provided the only way for Hildegard and women of her era to develop their intellectual, artistic, and spiritual talents as literate women, writers, teachers, healers, and leaders of communities (Mews 2004, p. 92). Hildegard embraced these opportunities without critique concerning the structures of female subordination in which she was steeped. Newman notes, "Hildegard did not call for radical change of the social or ecclesiastical structures; it was the abuse of authority, not the nature of it, she opposed" (*Scivias* 1990, p. 21).

The Lady Was a Bishop

Yet, again, Hildegard manages to affirm the prerogatives of men and, at the same time, imagine an alternative "with future content." In her *Scivias*, Hildegard writes, "Women should not approach the office of the altar" (Book II, vision 6, number 76). Women cannot be ordained because "they are an infirm and weak habitation, appointed to bear children and diligently nurture them." Yet, of course, Hildegard was herself an example of female capacity to transform feminine weakness into the locus of spiritual power. She places herself wearing Episcopal vestments in Vision 5 in the *Scivias* (see plate 9). She does this out of a prophetic necessity, not meaning to suggest an enduring sacramental vocation for the female. Her intent is to shock effeminate clergy into reawakening to the responsibilities of their call; yet somehow the image is so fitting to Hildegard herself. While Hildegard consistently argued that women ought not to consider the priestly office, she undertook four preaching missions with ecclesiastical approval. Again, this was due to the "womanish" clergy who no longer had *viriditas* and who forced her into roles preordained for them. When times would grow virile and masculine again, women would not have to be strong and could again assume their more submissive character.

In an article entitled "Hildegard of Bingen on Gender and the Priesthood," Augustine Thompson said: "Some have found her attitude a relic of 'cultural conservatism' or evidence of a deep inconsistency in her thought, where her 'theological symbolism' (that is positive about the feminine) clashes with inherited 'monastic theology' (that is negative about the feminine)" (1994, p. 350). I think Hildegard lived amid these tensions and while she experienced and admitted to a sense of female inferiority, she spoke and wrote with a confident self-assertion. It seems a given that without her appeal to divine inspiration, if she had not named her mission a prophetic one, Hildegard most certainly would not have gotten the affirmation of the church. Peter Dronke has suggested that as a prophet Hildegard assumed many high sacerdotal functions without serious opposition, such as preaching and exorcism, which in general the church has seen, and continues to see, as male prerogatives (Dronke 1984, p. 149). Hildegard used the prejudices of her day to her advantage. Tatiana Tsakiropoulou-Summers writes, "Hildegard's phenomenal success (and her appeal to modern readers) is due precisely to the fact that she upheld the social conventions and standards of her times while at the same time undermining them methodically through her actions" (in Churchill, Brown, and Jeffrey 2002, p. 134). An amazing facet of Hildegard's personality is her ability to exercise her will power to carve out creative avenues of expression in order to fulfill what she believed to be God's will for her life. I believe Carl Jung perceived this in Hildegard as strength of personality, complexity of mind and inner life, which enabled her to transcend the limits imposed on her as a female and to find the creative resources do to so with dignity and grace, and in the process achieve individuation. Had her boldness crossed a line into arrogance or destructive projection, she might have lost her voice of authority via the support she received from men with more power than she. Her pro-female activities countered the pejorative attitudes toward women's physical, intellectual, and ecclesial inferiority. Just imagine a sixty-something woman in her time traveling hundreds of miles on horseback or on foot to preach? She was indefatigable. The future entered her long before it happened.

> But this is a weak, womanly age, and
> the Church is neither as truthful nor as
> kind as it should be. However, God is at work.
> Like a female warrior, God fights to vanquish
> every type of unfairness on earth.
>
> —Hildegard, in a letter to the Prelates at Mainz,
>   1178 or 1179

Hildegard, Gender, and
Religious Leadership

In what ways, then, could Hildegard have relevance to the contemporary dialogue around gender and religious leadership today? I believe that because her behavior was prophetic and actually lived out by Hildegard, she reveals something about the nature of woman and the female capacity to be *in persona Spiritus Dei*. Prophecy, by nature, is a decisive break with the status quo. The Judeo-Christian prophetic tradition finds its prophets speaking on behalf of a God who is an advocate of the oppressed, an overturner of unjust orders, a God whose action in history points toward a new future, a reconstructed community. Biblical prophesy is seldom far from religious and political criticism. God is simultaneously the creator of religious and social institutions and the challenger of those same institutions, by inspiring persons, including women, to act critically on God's behalf in calling for institutional conversion in the direction of God's justice. Hildegard, a dangerous memory, has reemerged as a historical resource to address and redress our time of clerical abuse and moral failures in church and society precisely because she is such an apt example of a woman within this revered prophetic strand of religious tradition.[2]

So many examples have already been given of Hildegard's brilliant theology, her holistic worldview, and her positive appropriation of the feminine and female nature relative to the Divine. As stated on the end of the preceding chapter, I am led to wonder if the leap from being *in persona Spiritus Dei* is not so far from standing *in persona Christi*? *In persona Christi* means taking on the role of Christ to the point of being the very image of the Christ. Hildegard's theological anthropology does allow for the ontological possibility for the female to be *in persona Christi*, disclosing the capacity of female nature to "bear the grace of orders." According to Hildegard's prophetic visions and her anthropology, it is not abhorrent, philosophically and theologically speaking, for female nature to mediate the divine and to have the spiritual capacity to stand *in persona Christi*.

In this regard, an appeal to Hildegard is highly relevant, at least in the Roman Catholic Church, where dialogue on the subject of women and ordination is verboten. While the current "definitive" teaching says the church has no authority to confer ordination upon women as a matter of the deposit of faith, much is said about the symbolic necessity of maleness *in persona Christi* and the long-standing tradition of the church. Hidden underneath the argument from symbol and tradition is the deeper philosophical underpinning of female ontological incapacity to bear the grace of orders because of innate defectiveness. Hildegard is a striking counterpoint, a submerged tradition within the tradition, which suggests that the prophetic, actual, and historically verifiable activities of this twelfth-century abbess present us with a paradox. One way to characterize this paradox is to say that while Hildegard appeared to be in complicity with the gender expectations of her times, her lived witness to female potency and potentiality told another story. She meets Metz's definition of a dangerous memory. She broke the canon of all that was taken as self-evident and unmasked the deceptive certainty that the way things are, are the way they must remain. She did indeed subvert the structures of plausibility in anthropology, theology, music, art, healing, and more. Hildegard of Bingen is a dangerous memory of an incalculable visitant from the past with future content to be reckoned with in an emerging post-patriarchal twenty-first century. She is, as we will see, an animus woman.

Jung's Theory of Anima and Animus

In *Jung's Map of the Soul* (1998), Murray Stein synthesizes Jung's notion of anima and animus. In short, the anima is the feminine principle in a man's personality and the animus is the masculine principle in a woman's personality. Jung was convinced that both genders possess both masculine and feminine characteristics and qualities. Like Hildegard, Jung, as a European male, transcended the limits of his time, yet was shaped by the prevailing assumptions of the time in which he lived, which was emphatically patriarchal. Therefore, he is applauded for offering a vision of the integrated personality as needing the feminine aspect in healthy manhood and the masculine aspect in healthy womanhood. His identification of masculine and feminine characteristics, however, seems stereo-typical to our more evolved post-modern sensibility. At the same time, research on the psychology of gender, gender differences, and sex and social behavior is blossoming, evidencing widespread interest in the difference gender makes in psychological maturing.

Stein summarized Jung's position as follows:

> Jung says that men are masculine on the outside and feminine on the inside, and that women are the other way around. Women are relational and receptive in their ego and persona, and they are hard and penetrating on the other side of their personality; men are tough and aggressive on the outside and soft and relational within. Take away the personas of male and female adults, and the perception of gender will be reversed. Women will be harder and more controlling than men, and men will be more nurturing and relational like women. (1998, pp. 134–35)

The anima and animus are realities of the inner worlds of men and women—their hidden personalities, their unconscious other selves. When a woman becomes conscious of her animus and is able to integrate it successfully, she manifests, with a certain energy and dignity, exuberance, forthrightness, toughness, perseverance, and strength of spirit. When a man becomes conscious of his anima and is able to integrate it successfully, he manifests, with a certain tenderness and dignity, empathy, capacity for nurturance, mutuality and reciprocity in relationships, and appreciation for interdependence.

The contents of the anima and animus are constructed by society, culture, history, religion, and personal life experience, while the structure itself is stable through time and cultures; in other words, archetypal (Stein 1998, p. 186). I agree with Stein that it is this complexity and mysterious uniqueness in human beings that Jung was attempting to discern and which he describes in his theory of anima and animus. Some of the creative fruits of the feminist movement, sexual revolution, and developments in the science of psychology in the later part of the twentieth century and the early years of the new millennium have contributed to the lessening of gender polarization and overvaluation of stereotypical masculine qualities and the male principle. A renewed appreciation for animus in woman is emerging, with the possibility of turning it from problem to promise.

The complementary character of the anima
also affects the sexual character,
as I have proved to myself beyond a doubt.
A very feminine woman has a masculine soul,
and a very masculine man has a feminine soul.

—C. G. Jung, *Psychological Types,* par. 804

Masculine has been almost universally defined
by such adjectives as active, hard, penetrating,
logical, assertive, dominant;
feminine has been widely defined as
receptive, soft, giving, nourishing
relational, emotional, empathic.
The debate is whether these categories
should be associated with gender.

—Murray Stein, *Jung's Map of the Soul*

Animus in Hildegard

A woman who cooperates with her animus is a woman with character, substance, and discipline of thought and creativity. She distinguishes herself from an unconscious animus woman who is passive, intellectually fuzzy, lacking in distinctive personality, absent from her own self. Jane Hollister Wheelwright took up this question at a time when few were developing this Jungian concept specifically from a female perspective. In *For Women Growing Older: The Animus*, Wheelwright says,

> To this day when the animus finds its legitimate or creative expression, it seems to promote an unaccustomed fluency in painting, writing or whatever activity is undertaken. The woman believes in her female self and what she needs to express, and the animus supports her. Or, as liaison to her deep level of creative source, the animus dives down to bring up the inspired content she needs. (1984, p. 20)

It seems to me that Jung knew Hildegard was an animus woman different from his more limited conceptions. Jung's own perspective on animus in women was not sufficiently mature, somewhat negative, and dependent a woman's relationship to an actual man. Hildegard lived a celibate life surrounded by other women. It is true, however, that she maintained a long, trusted, and productive relationship with her monk-secretary Volmar that lasted more than thirty years. In addition, she experienced significant affiliations with men—mentors, secretaries, and superiors—who were supportive of her visions and her theological and ecclesial pioneering ventures. It is fair to say that these men, along with the environs of monastic life, constellated the creative animus in Hildegard. I believe Jung marveled at the scope and depth of Hildegard's creativity, novelty, recorporation of the feminine into the Godhead, ability to articulate the reality of the demonic in the human quest for spiritual wholeness, capacity to decipher the meaning of symbols, and the precision of her thinking. I am led to think that when Jung commented on Hildegard as "an outstanding personality quite apart from her mysticism" (1957, par. 42), he just might have been referring to a well-integrated animus that, for the most part, guided her diverse talents, boundless creativity, and undefeatable personality. In short, her self worked through a powerful animus in providing her the courage to be what she was.

Hildegard is a model of an animus woman, before Jung deemed it possible in a positive sense. The work of women analysts like Jane Wheelwright and churchwomen like Joan Chittister, OSB, have and are forging new conceptual depth to how the animus energy functions in today's woman (at least, in the North American context). Wheelwright suggested twenty years ago that we seek out certain older women who have not fit the patriarchally determined stereotypes and learn from their lives, in order to determine the stuff from which women are made. These are women whose actual lives suggest a new future. They seem to find an abundance of meaning, creative expression, energy, and the living through of life with few roads left untraveled.

In our time, animus women are among those now in their seventies, eighties, and nineties whose courageous choices, made long ago, to trouble and struggle opened doorways; they paid with their wombs, their sleep, their lives that we might walk through new gateways upright. They are the ones who understand the courage it takes to plumb the depths, when truth distilled from experience becomes wisdom. Christian history and the history of women religious in particular is replete with transformational persons of biblical proportions, the ones spoken of who pass into every generation as vessels of Holy Wisdom (Wisdom 7:21–28). They are the carriers of dangerous memory who emerge into every present with future content. Twelfth-century German Benedictine abbess Hildegard of Bingen and twenty-first-century Benedictine prioress Joan Chittister are but two such liminal, wise, plucky, and prophetic women.

"'Age puzzles me,' wrote Florida Scott-Maxwell, the Jungian psychologist, in her journal, *The Measure of My Days*, which she kept in her eighties. 'I thought it was a quiet time. My seventies were interesting and serene but my eighties are passionate. I grow more intense with age'" (Chittister 2008, p. 179). We may ask why women of a certain age continue to be stirred and to stir? We might answer: Because we need their passion now more than ever in a time of waning *viriditas*.

Humanity seems to have reached a point where the concepts of the
past are no longer adequate, and we begin to realize that our nearest
and dearest are actually strangers to us, whose language we no longer
understand. It is beginning to dawn on us that the people living on
the other side of the mountain are not made up exclusively of red-
headed devils who are responsible for all the evil on this side of the
mountain. A little of this uneasy suspicion has filtered through into
the relation between sexes; not everyone is utterly convinced that
everything good is in "me" and everything evil in "you." Already
we can find super-moderns who ask themselves in all seriousness
whether there may not be something wrong with us, whether perhaps
we are too unconscious, too antiquated, and whether this may
not be the reason why when confronted with difficulties in sexual
relationships we still continue to employ with disastrous results the
methods of the Middle Ages if not those of the caveman.

—C. G. Jung, *The Symbolic Life,* par. 1799

The critical principle of feminist theology is the
promotion of the full humanity of women.
Whatever denies, diminishes, or distorts the full
humanity of women is, therefore, appraised as
not redemptive. Theologically speaking, whatever
diminishes or denies the full humanity of women
must be presumed not to reflect the divine or to
reflect the authentic nature of things, or to be the
message or work of an authentic redeemer or a
community of redemption. This negative principle
also implies the positive principle: what does promote
the full humanity of women is of the holy, it does reflect
the true relation to the divine; it is the true nature
of things, the authentic message of redemption
and the mission of redemptive community.

—Rosemary Ruether, *Sexism and God-Talk*

In referring to the 1976 approbation of Pope Paul VI and the
"Declaration on the Admission of Women to the Ministerial
Priesthood," theologian Karl Rahner reported: "The Roman
declaration says that in this question the church must preserve
fidelity to Jesus Christ. That is in principle clearly correct. But
the question of what loyalty in this case actually consists of still
remains open . . . . This can be looked forward to with patience
and confidence. This patience, however, should not be overtaxed:
time is pressing, and one certainly cannot wait a century for the
church [to change] without damage."

—Karl Rahner, SJ, in *National Catholic Reporter*

Notes

1. See Macy 2006, pp. 16–32. In addition, Macy provides a listing of
the rites from the seventh through the eleventh centuries. The ordinals
from this period contain ceremonies for the ordination of deaconesses that
parallel that of deacons. The section that contains the rites for ordination
lists the following:
Ritual for ordaining a cleric
Ritual for ordaining a sacristan
Ritual for ordaining the person who is committed to the care of books
    and writing
Ritual over a person who wishes to cut his beard
Ritual for ordaining a subdeacon
Blessing for the consecration of the head cleric
Preface for ordaining a priest
Ritual for ordaining an archpriest
Ritual for ordaining an abbot
Blessings for a garment dedicated to God
Ritual for blessing of a virgin
Ritual or blessing for a veiled woman dedicated to God
Ritual for ordaining an abbess
(Macy 2008, p. 37, nn. 91, 175)

The argument for not accepting, for example, the "Ritual for the
Ordination of an Abbess" as a real ordination is to suggest it was more a sort

of blessing or commissioning and not a true ordination. Such discussion was part of Hildegard's era, and not long after her death most canonists and theologians began to interpret references to women's ordination in early Christian history as blessing ceremonies with no equivalency to male ordination to the presbyterate or deaconate. Macy says, "this remains a present day potent stratagem for denying the ordination of women in the past . . . [thereby] expunging the memory of ordained women from Christianity" (2008, pp. 99, 110). In addition, see Zagano 2000.

2. This is why when asked within whom her spirit is alive today that I respond: Sister Joan Chittister, OSB, as a preeminent witness for reform within the contemporary church.

Application

Relying on the notion of dangerous memory identified in this chapter as well as the model of Hildegard as an animus woman, retrieve the name and story of a woman who functions for you as a dangerous memory and as an example of the transformative power of an animus woman in your life or in our post-patriarchal times. If you wish, tell the story to another. Then spend some time journaling about the experience of retelling the story.

CHAPTER 7

Viriditas: Hildegard's Green Life Force

When you see aridity, make it green.

—Hildegard

The most fascinating part of Hildegard's work
is really her "cosmic theology,"
a vision of the universe
that is both vast and minute,
a dazzling view cast over the world.

—Régine Pernoud, *Hildegard of Bingen:*
Inspired Conscience of the 12th Century

When Yahweh created the world
from . . . the "Void," he could not
help breathing his own mystery
into the Creation which is
himself in every part. . . .
From this comes
the belief that it is possible
to know God from his Creation.

—C. G. Jung, *Answer to Job*

Behold, I make all things new.

—Revelation 21:5

Introduction

In setting out to work with Hildegard's most novel theological concept—*viriditas*, a notion at the heart of her ecological theology and spirituality—I experienced what Jung means by synchronicity—a meaningful coincidence—more than mere chance. You may recognize what I am referring to by these markers:

> when you stumble upon a book unread and long-forgotten and then another arrives just at the right time;

> when information offered by a friend who knew you were working on Hildegard as an early ecologist mysteriously falls out of a worn folder;

> when a website jotted on a napkin shows up as a bookmark in said unread long-forgotten book.

This synchronicity animated an awareness of the importance of Hildegard as a reclaimable resource within the Christian tradition in our time of ecological crises. I have now read *Gaia and God* by Rosemary Ruether (1992), which sat untouched for far too many years. I also read the newly published *Quest for the Living God* (2008) by Elizabeth A. Johnson. The worn folder revealed an outline for a course on the history of the eco-feminist/spirituality movement.[1] I also investigated the scrawling on the napkin that directed me to the futurist Peter Russell and his "world clock."

These discoveries and the long pause each provided influenced the shaping of this chapter celebrating Hildegard's prescience about things to come, and Jung's hints at an ecopsychology, namely his perspectives on the interpenetration of psyche, nature, and spirit providing an empathic link to holism. These resources arrived on the scene just when I needed them, and these unexpected forays widened and refined the lens for the following reflections on Hildegard's invention of *viriditas*, Jung's references to Hildegard in this regard, and the implications for a human consciousness needed now, one more expansive and more humble than ever before.

> The stunning world opened up by Big Bang cosmology
> and evolutionary biology on the one hand,
> and the vulnerability of life on Earth needing
> protection on the other, is leading ecological theology
> to glimpse the Spirit's presence and activity
> with new contours, as the living God who is
> source, sustainer and goal of the whole shebang.
>
> —Elizabeth Johnson, *Quest for the Living God*, p. 183

> In some way or other
> we are part of a single, all-embracing psyche.
>
> —C. G. Jung, "The Spiritual Problem of
> Modern Man," par. 175

The "*viriditas* thread" is evident in Hildegard's theological trilogy: beginning with her doctrinal work, the *Scivias*; through the *Book of Life's Merits*, begun in 1158 and completed in 1163; and finally, to the *viriditas* thread woven into her most mature work begun in 1163 and completed in 1173, the *Book of Divine Works*. This work reveals Hildegard's cosmology, with particular reference to the favored place of humanity in creation. What follows in these pages is a lengthy meditation on Hildegard's green vision of humanity in relation to the cosmos, and her sense of the interdependency and interconnectedness of, as she calls it, the "web of all life."

> O Holy Spirit,
> you are the mighty way in which everything
> that is in the heavens, on the earth and under the earth
> is penetrated with connectedness,
> penetrated with relatedness.
>
> —Hildegard, *Meditations with Hildegard of Bingen*

It is important to acknowledge two medical books written immediately following the completion of the *Scivias—The Book of Simple Medicine* or *Natural History*, also known as *Physica*, and *Causes and Cures*. *Physica* is a scientific discourse in which Hildegard explains all of nature's functions and subtleties as seen in her visions. *Causes and Cures* is a book on human health and healing. Only two medical books were written in the West in the twelfth century and both of these works are attributed to Hildegard.

This chapter includes insights arising from Victoria Sweet's *Rooted in the Earth, Rooted in the Sky: Hildegard of Bingen and Pre-Modern Medicine* (2006), the first book to use Hildegard's scientific texts to revise not only certain conceptions of Hildegard but also of pre-modern medicine itself. Schipperges has noted that no other medieval person came anywhere near Hildegard in grasping and articulating an understanding of the invisible web of nature or her universal empathy with all the elements of creation (1997, p. 63). It is widely accepted that Hildegard's visionary works established the foundation for modern creative thinkers in the later twentieth and early twenty-first centuries, developing an eco-spirituality based on the interdependence of all aspects of the created universe.

We know that all creation is groaning in labor pains
even until now; and not only that, but we ourselves,
who have the first fruits of the Spirit, we also
groan within ourselves as we wait for adoption, the
redemption of our bodies. For in hope we were saved.
Now hope that sees for itself is not hope. For who
hopes for what one sees? But if we hope for what we
do not see, we wait with endurance. In the same way,
the Spirit too comes to the aid of our weakness; for
we do not know how to pray as we ought, but the
Spirit itself intercedes with inexpressible groanings.
And the one who searches hearts knows what is
the intention of the Spirit, because it intercedes
for the holy ones according to God's will.

—Letter to the Romans 8:22–28

Even when one understands the logic of patriarchy as a conceptual framework and social system oppressive to women, it still seems amazing that Hildegard's remarkable scholarly opuses remained in relative obscurity until the later part of the twentieth century. Equally amazing is how relevant this twelfth-century abbess has been to the deep foundations of contemporary ecofeminism and the conviction that the environmental crisis is rooted in the spiritual crises of our time. Ecofeminism necessarily spawned ecofeminist spiritualities as a challenge to the domination of nature so key to patriarchy by unearthing deeper traditions beneath patriarchy that return to a nondominating and life-affirming belief system, values, behaviors, and relationships among humans toward nonhuman nature. Years ago, ecofeminists began to posit an empowering alliance between ecology and feminism as an antidote to the same dualistic thinking that split the masculine from the feminine, men from women, reason from emotion, spirit from matter, and soul from body.

In short, ecofeminism brings together ecology and feminism and explores how male domination of women and the domination of nature interconnect, both in cultural ideology and in social structures (Ruether 1992, p. 2). The rise of ecological consciousness, intimately related to the emergence of feminist and other liberationist movements, recognized that the whole of creation is on a sacred journey groaning for greening. Johnson reminds, "If the earth is a sacrament of divine presence, a locus of divine compassion, and a bearer of divine promise, then its ongoing destruction through ecocide, biocide, and geocide is deeply sinful desecration" (2008, p. 197). In addition, our consciousness is stretched to consider the great command of Jesus to love one another as extending its membership to all God's creatures, great and small: "'Who is my neighbor,' asks eco-theologian Brian Patrick Anthony, 'the Samaritan? The outcast? The enemy? Yes, of course. But it is also the whale, the dolphin, and the rain forest. Our neighbor is the entire community of life, the entire universe. We must love it all as our very self'" (ibid., p. 198).

Either the human community and its natural environs will go into the future as a single sacred community or both will perish in the desert of our ecologically destructive decision-making (see Berry

1991). Up to this point in evolutionary time, we have been trying to go into the future as a human community with an exploitative relationship to animals, nature, and natural resources without a deep sense of our shared integrity as a single sacred web of life. The patriarchal worldview operates in such as way as to provide those privileged by these power arrangements the ability to expand their power boundlessly, draining the lives of those deemed inferior or expendable as well as the natural resources of life upon which we all depend. This has finally resulted in civilization on a brink, which Hildegard foresaw and forewarned centuries ago.

When patriarchal spirituality associates women, body and nature and then emphasizes transcending the body and transcending the rest of nature, it makes oppression sacred.

—Carol Adams, *Ecofeminism and the Sacred*

It is important to note, as does Ruether in *Gaia and God*, that our experience of ecological crisis does not mean that previous eras in human history have not been at such a brink and even experienced large-scale annihilation. However, as long as populations remained small and human technology weak, these devastations were remediated by migration or adaptation of new sustainable techniques. The invention and use of the atomic bomb at Hiroshima and Nagasaki catapulted human consciousness to an awareness of the diabolical capacity of human ingenuity to destroy the planet through the exercise of our own power. The radical nature of this new face of ecological destruction within human means produced an unprecedented situation of human capacity for global catastrophe (Reuther 1992, p. 206). Physicist Robert Oppenheimer, supervising scientist of the Manhattan Project, is reported to have quoted the *Bhagavad-Gita* on July 16, 1945, as he witnessed the first atomic detonation in the New Mexican desert near the Trinity site in the White Sands Missile Range: "I am become Death, the shatterer of worlds." Einstein is reported to have had a similar thought: "The release of atom power has changed everything except our way of thinking . . . the solution to this problem lies in the heart of mankind. If only I had known, I should have become a watchmaker." Jung observed:

> Nowadays we can see as never before that the peril which threatens all of us comes not from nature, but from man, from the psyches of the individual and the mass. The psychic aberration of man is the danger. Everything depends upon whether or not our psyche functions properly. If certain persons lose their heads nowadays, a hydrogen bomb will go off. (1969, p. 132)

Jung perceived the connection between a growing technological and mechanized society and dehumanization. When contact with nature became more and more distant for the modern person, gone with it was the "profound emotional energy that this symbolic connection supplied" (Jung 1964, p. 95). On the danger of the disassociation of humans from nature, Jung said, "This explains our many relapses into the most appalling barbarity, and it also explains the really terrible fact that, the higher we climb the mountain of scientific and technical achievement, the more dangerous and diabolical becomes the misuse of our inventions" (1939, par. 1009).

Everything now depends on man: immense power of destruction is given into his hand, and the question is whether he can resist the
    will to use it,
and can temper his will with the spirit of love and wisdom.
He will hardly be capable of doing so on his own unaided
    resources.
He needs the help of an "advocate" in heaven.

—C. G. Jung, *Answer to Job,* par. 745

The threats to survival have remained unabated since the advent of atomic and nuclear power. Daily personal and collective behaviors damage a fragile ecosystem, depleting life on land and in the sea and the air we breathe. Twenty percent of people who inhabit the earth—North Americans—use seventy-five percent of the world's resources to meet their seemingly insatiable needs, all the while thinking of ourselves as the most generous people on the globe. Threats to human and planetary existence have accelerated in their ominous prevalence in a time where the term "unprecedented" is used on a regular basis to describe nature and the exercise of human freedom seemingly gone awry in "natural" disasters like Katrina and what we simplistically call "9-11." Western civilization is struggling into a new way of thinking in an era that is post-patriarchal, in need of an earth-healing that must begin with personal and societal transformation. As Ruether says, "We need to transform our inner psyches and the way we symbolize the interrelation of men and women, humans and the earth, humans and the divine, the divine and the earth. Ecological healing is a theological and psychic-spiritual process" (1992, p. 4).

The unholy litany is well known:
global warming, holes in the ozone layer,
clear-cut forests, drained wetlands, denuded soils,
polluted air, poisoned rivers, overfished oceans,
and, over all, the threat of nuclear conflagration.

—Elizabeth Johnson, *Quest for the Living God*

Not only do I leave the door open for the Christian message,
but I consider it of central importance for Western man.
It needs, however, to be seen in a new light, in accordance
with the changes wrought by the contemporary spirit.

—C. G. Jung, *Memories, Dreams, Reflections*, p. 210

I answer for the ancestors
the questions their lives once
left behind.

—C. G. Jung, *Memories, Dreams, Reflections*, p. 237

Yet another book on Hildegard, like this one, is the persistent effort to raise to consciousness a previously submerged strand of the Christian tradition so that her medieval and timeless voice continues as an urgent cry for a new future whose destiny we hold within us. While the aims of this book transcend denominationalism, both Hildegard and Jung lived within the Christian story. Jung maintained the conviction that "Christianity has shown us the way, but, as the facts bear witness, it has not penetrated deeply enough below the surface" (1948, par. 455). A critical mass of the more than one billion Christians of the world might be spurred into an ecological consciousness if they can finally feel the burn of new claims as gospel imperatives for the time that is ours. We will never find the whole of what we are seeking neatly waiting for rediscovery in any past tradition, but we rediscover and appropriate touchstones for authentic life still alive in ancient sources, like eternal springs that never run dry and quench today's thirst just as they did for generations before we arrived. Mining the past is like digging for the roots that nourish in the midst of the wilderness. Out of this quest, one can assemble a vision of "good news" and practical pathways to life that can be articulated for today (Ruether 1992, p. 365). As Jung wisely noted, one way of living is not easily abandoned unless it is exchanged for another whose legitimacy is compelling (1969, p. 166). Hildegard's inconvenient truth, once eclipsed, reemerges.

If human beings abuse their position of power
over the rest of God's creation, then God
will allow other creatures to rise up and
punish them. Do not regard other creatures
as existing merely to serve your bodily needs.
By cherishing them as God requires,
your soul will benefit.

—Hildegard, *Book of Divine Works*, 3.2

In the *Book of Divine Works,* Hildegard
offers Western civilization a deep and healing
medicine for what may well be its number-one
disease of the past few centuries: *anthropocentrism.*

—Matthew Fox, *Hildegard of Bingen's Book of Divine Works*

We need a worldview characterized by ecocentricity,
rather than egocentricity.

—Jeremy Yunt, "Jung's Contribution to an Ecological Psychology," p. 119

Hildegard, Nature, and All Things Material

When one thinks about the long historical sweep of Christianity,
one inevitably confronts the rather negative attitude toward the
material world that became endemic to the Western Christian
tradition. The word *nature* in Western thought was and is a problem.
Ruether comments:

> The word nature is used in four distinct senses in Western
> culture: (1) as that which is "essential" to a being; (2) as the sum
> total of physical reality, including humans; (3) as the sum total
> of physical reality apart from humans; and (4) the "created"
> world apart from God and divine grace. (1992, p. 5)

The patriarchal paradigm that shaped Western consciousness
for millennia evolved in such a way that humans were viewed as
over against all that is nonhuman, and thus developed a concept
of nature as both the nonhuman and the nondivine. In dominant
Christianity, the material world is rife with sources of temptation.
The things of the world, of baser nature, have a tendency to pull
the dominant male away from his higher being. In this hierarchical
and dualistic construct, the female became associated with matter,
nature, and sexuality and fell clearly on the negative and weak side
of the dualistic continuum of value and power. In this worldview,
the purpose of other aspects of the created universe—animals,

minerals, and plants—existed solely at the service of the more rational creatures. Man, specifically meaning elite males, controlled and dominated nature for his use.

"See," Ochwiay Biano said, "how cruel the whites look. . . .
We do not know what they want. We do not understand them.
We think that they are mad."
   I asked him why he thought the whites were all mad.
   "They say that they think with their heads," he replied.
   "Why of course. What do you think with?" I asked him in surprise.
   "We think here," he said, indicating his heart.
   I fell into a long meditation.

—C. G. Jung, *Memories, Dreams, Reflections,* p. 247–48

Hildegard was one of the few Christian writers in the medieval period who rejected this attitude and put forward a vision of God's creativity as imbuing all aspects of creation with sacred mystery. As Schipperges puts it, the subject of the *Book of Divine Works* is the unity of the order of creation. Nature and grace, body and spirit, body and soul, world and the church—everything is in harmony and glorifies unanimously the Creator (Fox, in *Illuminations,* p. 43). There is no ambiguity toward the whole of creation in Hildegard, no revulsion of the earthly, bodily, or inanimate nature. She does not see the natural world as inherently evil or corrupting. Unlike the writings of many Christian thinkers and mystics before and since, the person seeking sanctity is not required to escape the natural world. Hildegard wrote, "Holy persons draw to themselves all that is earthly." For her, the natural world was not an arena of chaos that humans must either avoid or do battle with in order to dominate or domesticate. Hildegard said:

As the Creator loves his creation, so creation loves the Creator. Creation, of course, was fashioned to be adorned, to be showered, to be gifted with the love of the Creator. The entire world has been embraced by this kiss. God has gifted creation with everything that is necessary. (Uhlein 1983, p. 51)

Examples are replete in *Simple Medicine* or *Natural History,* a text in which Hildegard explores everything from gemstones and healing to female sexual desires and the physiology of conception in support of her position on the earth as a living divinized organic system. She says, "In all creation, in trees, plants, animals and stones—there are hidden secret powers which no one can discern until they are revealed by God" (Van de Weyer 1997, p. 34). She goes on to say, since "human beings cannot live without the rest of nature, so they must care for all natural things" (ibid., p. 42). In this regard, Hildegard goes so far as to speculate that humans, created in God's own image, exist not *to use* creation but *to serve* creation, precisely because of their abilities to partner with one another in intelligent, just, and caring relation to and in creation. "God created all things," Hildegard says in the *Scivias* 3.1.1:

> fashioning all things to reflect his glory. All creatures by their very nature worship God, honoring him as their creator. Even the stones under your feet worship God, for hidden within every stone is a divine spirit. The true purpose of every creature has been ordained by God. (1997, p. 39)

From the *Book of Divine Works* she writes, "Throughout all eternity God wanted to create human beings, because he wanted partners in his task of creation" (p. 40). In short, human beings are creations of God (*opus Dei*); men and women realize themselves in relationship with each other and all aspects of creation (*opus alternum per alterum*); and they have an ecological and therapeutic task that arises from within their very essence (*opus cum creatura*) (Craine 1997, p. 72). Hildegard was far ahead of her time in thinking and living green.

There is a power in eternity,
and it is green.

—Hildegard

Men and women are the
light green heart of the
living fullness of nature.

—Hildegard

Viriditas

There is no way to pursue Hildegard's eco-spirituality without attention to her most popular and unique of theological creations: the concept of *viriditas*. Simply put, *viriditas* is the principle of all life, of all reality, emblematic of growth and fertility in all aspects of nature. The well-known medievalist Constant Mews notes:

> Only through reading the Latin text did I realize how frequently Hildegard alluded to the concept of *viriditas*, translated by Hart and Bishop in a wide range of ways: "freshness," "greenness," "vitality," "fecundity," and so on. I was particularly pleased to discover that this concept, rarely used by Augustine in his major theological treatises, was in fact a favourite notion of Gregory the Great. Instead of making broad brush claims about Hildegard's theology as "creation-centred" rather than "fall-redemption centred," I came to appreciate the subtlety of her debt to a patristic tradition that was more complex than often presented. (2004, p. 84)

Viriditas, a concept that most creatively captures the importance of color in Hildegard's rich symbolism, means the greening power of all creation: the green life force of the world. To be green or greening is to be in the state of grace, in the condition of being most receptive to the divine presence in creation and in humanity. *Viriditas* is linked to fertility and fecundity. Creation is greened though the mystery of dew and moisture. The "wetness" of *viriditas* was essential to life in both spiritual and earthly realms. *Viriditas* was associated with the Holy Spirit, "the green-giver of life." In the *Scivias*, Hildegard wrote, "Through the Word, the sweet moisture of holiness fell from God and in the Holy Spirit." Jesus is "green wood." *Viriditas* is the moistening nurture for all growth and an aspect of the divine order. It bears a natural resemblance to the verdant look of creation: the greening of creation mirrors the greening of the human soul (see figure 12).

The soul, in Hildegard's language, was compared with moisture drawn from the earth. In the *Book of Divine Works*, Hildegard called the soul the green life force of the flesh (Vision 4:21). The soul is what makes one alive from within. She said, "The soul is the green life-force of the flesh, for the body grows and prospers through her, just as the earth becomes fruitful when moistened. The soul humidifies the body so that it does not dry out, just like the rain which soaks into the earth" (ibid.). As Craine notes, in Hildegard's understanding "the macrocosm of the universe and the microcosm of human being, body and soul, are both energized by *viriditas,* the fecundity that has its source in God and in human response" (1997, p. 41).

God has imprinted on the soul
of every human being
the image of the world
as God wants it to be.

—Hildegard, *Book of Divine Works,* 1.2

In Hildegard's vision, the entire cosmos is God's dwelling place and humans are created to use their rationality and all their senses to maintain the balance needed for a healthy organism. The macrocosmic organism of the earth and the microcosmic organism of human beings were essentially interrelated. In the *Book of Life's Merits,* Hildegard made the point that "everything that exists in the order of God responds to the other" (Craine 1997, p. 66). This oft-quoted line from Hildegard underscores her conviction of the interrelatedness of all life. One of the principles underscored in the *Book of Life's Merits* is that people are not only responsible for the quality of their personal lives, but for one another, for their social and religious lives, and the well-being of the entire cosmos:

> Then I heard air, earth, water and fire complain to the tall cosmic man who wore the wind and earth's greenness:
> We can no longer do what God ordained us to do. We want to finish the journey He gave us, but we can't. We would run like we were meant to, if we could. But humans mistreat us. They abuse us. That is why we smell so horribly. That is why

we're black with pollution and teeming with plagues. Is there no justice in the world? No order?

The cosmic man said:

I'll cleanse you with My broom. I'll also put humanity on trial, until they repent. And they will. Whenever you're contaminated, I'll cleanse you by punishing those who pollute you. Can anyone belittle me? See? When people don't follow My teachings and learn to speak with divine honesty, then the air (like the breath accompanying their unholy words) is bad. Greenness also withers when humans pervert my teachings, saying, "How can we know a Lord we've never seen?"

But I say to them, "Don't you see Me day and night? Don't you see Me when you plant crops, and when your seeds are nurtured with rainwater? All of creation has an affinity for its Creator and knows the one Person made it. Only people rebel. Seek God in the books His wisdom made, and get reacquainted with your Creator (from the *Book of Life's Merits*, quoted in Butcher 2007, pp. 147–48).

It is not too great a leap of imagination to hear in these words recorded more than eight hundred years ago reference to our situation today of ecological devastation, acid rain, toxic waste, dying forests, and pollution of all kinds. Matthew Fox is quoted on this point as saying, "the Cosmos keeps a ledger—not God; and cosmic order will not in the long run tolerate human greed, human indifference to its beauties and its laws of balance and harmony" (in McDonagh 1986, p. 189).

If meanwhile, we give up the green vitality of these virtues
and surrender to the drought of our indolence,
so that we do not have the sap of life and the greening
    power of good deeds,
then the power of our very soul will begin to fade and dry up.

—Hildegard, *Illuminations*

More than a Metaphor

The preceding reflections summarize what some thoughtful medievalists and theologians think Hildegard meant by *viriditas*. More recently, Victoria Sweet, in her continuing study of the medicine of Hildegard of Bingen, probed deeply into two questions: We know what we, as moderns, mean by being green, but what did Hildegard really mean? Was Hildegard's *viriditas* more than a metaphor?[2] Clearly for Hildegard the notion of *viriditas* originated in the garden; it arose from what she grew. *Viriditas* began in her mind and imagination as a physical property: green sap. From the beginning, it was more than a metaphor. She uses the term in a special way as the "living power in which the power of the world is made manifest." *Viriditas* was not an abstraction for Hildegard, but a biological reality discovered from observation, which she imbued with meaning about the earth, humanity, the soul, personal and social ethics, physical health, the life of the church, and many other applications.

While Hildegard took the notion of *viriditas* to new depths and heights, she drew on the tradition of *viriditas* that was common in ancient sources available to her. The concept was used in spiritual life as a metaphor for growth and for the virtuous life, as an element with physical properties, such as those found in emeralds, and to denote the simple green of nature, as the fields, trees, and meadows are green. Contained in the idea of green is also the notion that some greens are dangerous, such as the green of unripe apples or pond scum; there is the physical reality of gangrene and the internal vexation of being green with envy. Sweet believes that for Hildegard, *viriditas* was all of this and more than a metaphor.

Behind the virtuous quality that *viriditas* most nobly signifies, there is, according to Sweet, the reality of *viriditas* as green fluid. This green fluid is that source of life hidden below the earth in the roots of things waiting to move up from the roots in spring, when rain moistens the earth, trees bear flowers, leaves, and fruit, and stems give forth fresh growth. *Viriditas* is fertile juice that lives first in the roots beneath the earth and then moves up to moisten and transform the stem to flower or vine to fruit. *Viriditas* is a force that produces a form of life: plant, tree, and flower. Hildegard believed that plants suck *viriditas* from roots buried deep in the earth. Behind the use of *viriditas* as animating metaphor is an actual substance: green sap or liquid that has a transforming and transformative effect not only in nature but also upon humans. This is where, according to Sweet (2008), Hildegard's application of the notion becomes unique.

Hildegard applies the biological notion of *viriditas* not only to natural phenomena but also to the human being—the human body. The word *viriditas* comes from two Latin words that mean raw life force and full of sap and energy. Hildegard does something special with the word *viriditas* precisely because she sees it within the human body as both metaphor and substance. For example, for Hildegard, the female flow of blood is not a source of that which is unclean but a sign of the *viriditas* of female biology. Woman's physicality is vibrant with life-giving properties that arise from her God-given nature. In turn, and with a different twist from the biology of her time, she sees the male seed, when it cooperates with female vitality, is strong and potent, as *viriditas*. Both men and women possess the green and greening source. In the ancient mindset, all created things consisted of mixtures of four elements: hot/cold or wet/dry—*viriditas* is hot and wet, thereby reflecting balance. Hozeski reminds, "Since the balance of the elements and their corresponding humors determined good or bad health in people, it was important to know the elemental qualities of plants. People could then determine their effect on persons who ate or used them—that is, in a balanced or unbalanced state" (*Hildegard's Healing Plants*, p. xii). *Viriditas* is essential to a vital, healthy human life, spiritual, social, and especially, ecclesial. For example, in talking about Christian baptism, Fox notes, "Our baptism is not a baptism *through* water but *into* moisture. It is a commitment on our part to stay wet and green. Like God" (*Illuminations,* p. 33). There is no aspect of living that is potentially devoid of *viriditas* because of its centrality to *all* life.

According to Hildegard, there was a certain chain of being: life from God is transmitted into plants, animals, and precious gems. People, in turn, eat plants and animals and acquire gems, thereby attaining *viriditas*. People express *viriditas* by practicing the virtues, and the life cycle of *viriditas* continues in unbroken rhythm

(Hozeski 1994, pp. xiii-xiv). Sweet asserts that the premodern body was more like a plant than a machine or a computer program, and the physician more like a gardener than a mechanic or a computer programmer. This logic is part of the distinctive feature of *viriditas* for Hildegard: the natural transformative process and properties of *viriditas* in the earth organically fills the human body and soul with *viriditas*. There is a sacramental quality to Hildegard's understanding of *viriditas* in that it effects what it signifies. This ancient notion of *viriditas* is part of the deep tradition, when recovered, that can assist the developing new human/earth-healing consciousness required for planetary survival in a new time.

When the elements from which the world is
made work in harmony, the soil is healthy,
the trees yield abundant fruit, the fields
yield abundant harvests, and all are happy.
But if the elements do not work in harmony,
the world becomes sick. The same applies
to human beings. If the elements from
which humans are made work in harmony,
the body and mind are healthy; but if they are
disharmonious, the body and mind become sick.

—Hildegard of Bingen, *Causes and Cures*, Vision 49:40

Hildegard's worldview was an artistic, socially charged, natural worldview, sustained by a spiritual mysticism. The cosmos and humankind are in a covenantal, reciprocal relationship. "Creation looks on its Creator like the beloved looks on the lover," so Hildegard writes (Gottfried and Theodoric 1995, p. 14). Hildegard also applied this notion as a way of pointing out what was wrong with the church in her era. She sensed that the essence of *viriditas*, critical to the Trinitarian life and the flow of right relations between humanity and the cosmos, were "drying up." She rails in one of her preaching tours, "The masters and prelates sleep without troubling themselves any more about justice . . . You should be day but you are night . . . you wish to have glory without merit and merit without work" (Pernoud 1998, pp. 138,144–45). The lack of *viriditas* within the power brokers of the church prompted Hildegard to speak and write boldly about reform as verdancy and refreshment. She said, "If meanwhile, we give up the green vitality of these virtues and surrender to the drought of our indolence, so that we do not have the sap of life and the greening power of good deeds, then the power of our very soul will begin to fade and dry up" (quoted in Gunn and Kelly 1999, p. 72). Because the priests, and prelates and princes, were "drying up," the likes of the "poor and frail" Hildegard and other mystics of her time were called by God to admonish them to authentic virility. Ever hopeful, she exhorts the clergy, "At this time, may the inextinguishable fire of the Holy Spirit fill you, so that you might convert to the best way" (Pernoud 1998, p. 166).

God's soul is the wind rustling pants and leaves,
the dew dancing on the grass,
the rainy breezes making everything to grow.
Just like this, the kindness of a person flows, touching
those dragging burdens of longing.
We should be a breeze helping the homeless,
dew comforting those who are depressed,
the cool, misty air refreshing the exhausted,
and with God's teaching we have got to feed the hungry:

This is how we share God's soul.

—Hildegard, *Hymn*

Foray into Jung

In *Answer to Job*, Jung makes a striking statement about God not being able to do anything other than to breathe God's own mystery into the Creation "which is himself in every part, as every reasonable theology has long been convinced. From this comes the belief that it is possible to know God from his Creation" (1952, par. 630). No doubt, Jung's own appreciation for the natural world influenced his sense of the pervasive presence of the divine. When he came up against a blank wall in his thinking, he painted a picture or hewed stone. In reference to an inscription carved in stone on one of the doorways at his home in Küsnacht, Jung says, "I put the inscription there to remind my patients and myself: *Timor dei initium sapientiae*" (The fear of the Lord is the beginning of wisdom). He went on to say of the meaning of crossing the threshold to therapy, "Here another no less important road begins, not the approach to 'Christianity' but to God himself and this seems to be the ultimate question" (in Jaffé 1979, p. 139).

Jung lamented the impoverishment of spirit that came along with the modern era. His directives to live by water, sail, work and explore outdoors, and hew the stone of Bollingen tower are all signposts of his resistance to materialism and rationalism, in which all the *numina* disappeared from the realm of nature and, in the process, estranged the human being from connection to his or her natural, spiritual essence. He writes, "At Bollingen I am in the midst of my true life, I am most deeply myself. . . . At times I feel as if I am spread out over the landscape . . . and am myself living in every tree, in the plashing of the waves, in the clouds and the animals that come and go, in the procession of the seasons" (1969, pp. 225–26). These insights and Hildegard's resonate with Alice Walker's indelible line: "I knew that if I cut a tree, my arm would bleed" (Shug to Celie, in *The Color Purple*, p. 178).

I have done without electricity, and tend the fireplace and stove myself. Evenings, I light the old lamps. There is no running water, and I pump the water from the well. I chop the wood and cook the food. These simple acts make man simple; and how difficult it is to be simple!

In Bollingen, silence surrounds me almost audibly, and I live "in modest harmony with nature."

—C. G. Jung, *Memories, Dreams, Reflections,* p. 226

Jung foreshadowed ecopsychology in realizing that humans needed to confront and reconcile a dilemma: "The tempo of the development of consciousness through science and technology was too rapid and left the unconscious, which could no longer keep up with it, far behind, thereby forcing it into a defensive

position which expresses itself in a universal will to destruction"
(1950b, par. 617). It would only be through an encounter with
the unconscious that the human psyche could probe the depths
as to how rational creatures could allow the beauty and integrity
of the world to become increasingly depreciated to the point of
threatening its own life support system—the biosphere, Gaia (Yunt
2001, p. 105).

Jung refers to Hildegard in *Psychology and Religion: West and East*
in the context of addressing those not of the Christian faith "but
those many people for whom the light has gone out, the mystery has
faded, and God is dead" (1940, par. 148).[3] Here, Jung resonates with
Christian theologian Wolfgang Pannenberg, who said, "Religions
die when their lights fail," that is, when their teachings no longer
illuminate life as it is actually lived (Johnson 2008, p. 23). In this
context, Jung considers ancient texts that refer to the spirit found
in natural phenomenon. He says:

> This spirit, coming from God, is also the cause of the "greenness,"
> the *benedicta viriditas*, much praised by the alchemists. . . . In
> Hildegard of Bingen's Hymn to the Holy Ghost, which begins "O
> ignis Spiritus paraclite," we read: "From you the clouds rain down,
> the heavens move, the stones have their moisture, the waters
> give forth streams, and the earth sweats out greenness." (1940,
> par. 151)

Here is Jung's appreciation of *viriditas*. One could speculate that
Jung relished the discovery of *viriditas* in Hildegard's theology
and cosmology because it fit so well with his convictions on the
interpenetration of the psyche, nature, and spirit, and human
potentiality for becoming whole. Jung said, "In some way or
other we are part of a single, all-embracing psyche" (1931, par.
175).

While *viriditas* is not a concept widely integrated into Jung's
work, this simple reference suggests Hildegard in the background
of Jung's processes of exploring the livingness of the eternal Spirit
abounding in nature and abiding in the human soul.[4] In this regard,
I have concluded something about Jung's relationship to Hildegard
that is based on his insight:

The difference between most people and myself is that for
me the "dividing walls" are transparent. That is my peculiarity.
Others find these walls so opaque that they see nothing behind
them and therefore think nothing is there. To some extent I
perceive the processes going on in the background, and that
gives me an inner certainty. (1969, p. 355)

Jung possessed an intuitive sense of the green sap of life residing
and hiding beneath consciousness. The inner compulsion to draw
it up from the unconscious was the most profound quest of his life.
Hildegard was not a passing fancy for Jung, but a figure present
to him through the decades, in the background, as a verdant inner
ancestor, scientist, and seer.

Mysterium Coniunctionis, Jung's last great work, in which he was
engaged for more than a decade from 1941 to 1954 (he finished
it in his eightieth year), provides another reference to Hildegard.
In section 6, "On the Conjunction," Jung discusses the symbolism
of water and water bearers, such as clouds and dew, as images
found in many ancient texts, and here again Hildegard appears,
in a lengthy footnote: "'From thee the clouds flow,' says Hildegard
of Bingen of the Holy Ghost" (1955–56, par. 727, note 173). The
footnote continues, linking Hildegard's use of the symbols of
clouds, rain, and dew as spiritually rich conveyors of meaning.
One of the principles that seems to pervade both Hildegard's
and Jung's discoveries regarding human spiritual potentiality is
that mystical experience is organic and native, exceptional only
in regards to its intensity, not in respect to its natural availability
in the human stretching toward greenness. Without naming it
so, both Hildegard's and Jung's eco-consciousness contribute to
today's quest for an ecological spirituality that will heal our one-
sidedness by pressing human consciousness to embrace the whole
web of interconnections. Our life on earth depends on righting
our relationships in the direction of becoming sustainers and not
destroyers of all that is given into our care. It is no accident that
nature's manifest greening power became a mirror image of the
greenness that lay hidden in the soul and in all eternity. This is why
Hildegard could say, "There is a power in eternity, and it is green"
(Schipperges 1997, p. 67).

> Enter by the narrow gate. The gate is
> wide and the road easy that leads to
> destruction and many choose to travel it.
> Narrow is the gate and difficult the road
> that leads to life, and few find it.
>
> —Matthew 7:13–14

> Deep calls to deep
> in the roar of your waterfalls;
> all your waves and breakers
> have swept over me.
>
> —Psalm 42:7

The Road to Our Depth: Implications for Greening in Our Time

What conclusions can be drawn from this venture back in time in order to live more authentically now in the time that is ours? Is there more to thinking green or going green than the sloganeering of the first decade of the twenty-first century? Ruether suggests that the search for an authentic ecological culture and society demands three elements: "(1) the rebuilding of primary and regional communities, in which people can understand and take responsibility for the ecosystem of which they are a part, (2) just relations between humans that accept the right of all members of the community to an equitable share in the means of subsistence; and (3) an overcoming of the culture of competitive alienation and domination for compassionate solidarity" (Ruether 1992, p. 201). These are sound ideas for the basis of a post-patriarchal, earth-healing, ethically mature approach to those new ways of thinking we need in order to live differently if the planet is to survive.

I believe that, after thousands and millions
of years, someone had to realize that this
wonderful world of mountains and oceans,
suns and moons, galaxies and nebulae, plants
and animals, *exists*. From a low hill in the
Athi plains of East Africa I once watched the
vast herds of wild animals grazing in soundless
stillness, as they had done from time immemorial,
touched only by the breath of a primeval world.
I felt then as if I were the first man, the first creature,
to know that all this *is*. The entire world round
me was still in its primeval state; it did not know
that it *was*. And then, in that one moment in
which I came to know, the world sprang into
being; without that moment it would never
have been. All Nature seeks this goal and
finds it fulfilled in man, but only in the most
highly developed and most fully conscious man.
Every advance, even the smallest, along this path
of conscious realization adds that much to the world.

—C. G. Jung, "Psychological Aspects of the Mother Archetype," par. 177

If you share the perspectives of this book—that we live in half-consciousness and are either dreadfully afraid or even oblivious to our time of peril—then you are, as both Hildegard and Jung would affirm, different from most people. If you accept that the masses of people on earth and the earth itself is in crisis, then any sincere, intelligent, studied approach to diagnosis might just lead to a treatment plan that results in the restoration of *viriditas* to address and redress the drying and dying out around and within us. There is, of course, both danger and opportunity in moving from sickness to health. We become responsible, in new ways, to work a program of living more consciously. Hildegard and Jung knew and embraced the costs of conscious living. We gather *the courage to be* in the face of our limits, our realistic imperfections, our guilt, grandiosity, anxiety, and emptiness. We see as if for the first time that our limits and illusions are inherent in our being-in-existence, and in the midst of that confrontation with our ego, finite time is invaded by eternity (Sayers 2003, p. 119).

We are grasped by something larger than the lure to power, accomplishment by outer standards, domination, and personal and collective self-absorption. It's just not all about *me* or *us* or what *we* are grasping after. We are not the graspers but the grasped. This is the moment of faith: the *kairos*. Life is and always will be about danger and opportunity, about risk to buck the tides of profit and acquisition and choose the life that flows from empathy, mutuality, self-donating love, and accountability.

The New Monastic Option

Thus, the metaphor of the narrow way found in the Christian scriptures is a powerful path to life-affirming, earth-healing, and life-sustaining Spiritual Presence. In his masterful work, *The Shaking of the Foundations*, Paul Tillich, a theologian deeply influenced by Jungian depth psychology, recommended sixty years ago the narrow path toward spiritual depth:

> The wisdom of all the ages and of all the continents speaks about the road to our depth. It has been described in innumerably different ways. But all those who have been concerned—mystics and priests, poets and philosophers, simple people and educated people—with that road through confession, lonely self-scrutiny, internal and external catastrophes, prayer, contemplation, have witnessed to the same experience. They have found that they were not what they believed themselves to be, even after a deeper level had appeared to them below the vanishing surface. That deeper level itself became surface, when a still deeper level was discovered, this happening again and again, as long as their very lives, as long as they kept on the road to their depth . . . .
>
> We live in history as much as our individual lives . . . the stream of daily news; the waves of daily propaganda, and the tides of conventions and sensationalism keep our minds occupied. The noise of these shallow waters prevents us from listening to the

sounds out of the depth . . . the cries of the social depths as they
are the cries out of the depths of our own souls . . . the depth of
suffering is the door [the gate], the only door, to the depth of
truth . . . Do not say that this is too profound . . . It is not too
profound, but rather because it is too uncomfortable, that you
shy away from the truth (Tillich 1948, pp. 56–57, 59–60).

What if we chose today, one by one, relationship by relationship,
family by family, school by school, and community by community
the road to our depth? We live within a culture at a turning point,
on a brink, rife with troubles and enormous energy for creativity or
destruction. What about the possibility of exploring Morris Berman's
notion of the "monastic option for the twenty-first century" (see
Berman 2000, pp. 132–58)? The *new monastic individual* (NMI),
in Berman's vision, lives beneath the currents of daily news, the
waves of daily propaganda, and the tides of conventions and
sensationalism. The noise of these shallow waters is monastically
resisted by the NMI, who disciplines herself or himself to listen
to the sounds arising from the Depth . . . the cries of the social
depths as they are the cries out of the depths of our own souls
. . . the depth of suffering is the door [the gate], the only door,
to the depth of truth. This individual gradually, without showy or
heroic effort, becomes a vehicle for a healthy culture. According to
Berman, new monastic individuals may have a profound impact
over time without intending to contribute to cultural evolution,
but certainly making a conscious choice not to be complicit in
narcissistic cultural devolution. I believe this is the impulse behind
Benetvision and Sister Joan Chittister's "point of view with the
future in mind"(www.benetvision.org). To provide resources that
will give depth and meaning in the midst of change and confusion.
In time, it will be the aggregate that will turn the tide.

There just might be an inner monk/nun, abbot or abbess, hiding
and residing in each of us. What might this mean for us? How might
this change our way of thinking about our spiritual capacities? The
Gospel of Luke records Jesus saying to his followers, "The Kingdom
of God is within you" (Luke 17:21). Some prefer the translation:
"The Kingdom of God is among you." Either way, what part of
this message don't we get? Paul Tillich said that it is not that such a

message is too profound, but rather because it is too uncomfortable, that we shy away from its summons upon our lives.

> [M]ost people find it quite beyond them
> to live on close terms with the unconscious.
> Again and again I have had to learn
> how hard this is for people.
>
> —C. G. Jung, *Memories, Dreams, Reflections*, p. 228

Are there twenty-first-century guides among us who can illuminate contemporary ways of being monastic? They actually abound. They are most likely to be those whose messages you most resist. Religious traditions by nature revere the great legacies preserved and transmitted that have sustained and ignited souls to new depths generation upon generation. Hildegard is one such trustable guide from the distant past and Jung another from the near past. Both visionaries challenge us to address what we so readily neglect: the inner impulses that beckon us to new growth and its life-giving and life-saving possibilities. We must resist the tendency, as understandable as it is, to slide past the claim of today's urgencies and take the trouble and time to reflect on what it is we must be and do, letting the ethical claims rest upon our hearts.

According to Robert L. Moore, we have intellectual, psychological, and spiritual resources for consciously confronting and regulating the grandiosity that is literally suffocating the life from us. In his book, *Facing the Dragon*, he offers for consideration his twenty-six "Dragon Laws in Personal Life," which invite the reader to explore where grandiose energies are active (2003, pp. 199–217).

> When medieval mapmakers came to the limit of their knowledge
> of the known world, they oftimes wrote in the empty space,
> "Here be dragons."
>
> —Elizabeth A. Johnson, *Quest for the Living God*

It is time to find, and if necessary fight, our way back to a sabbath from all the busyness that fills our days. The book *Busier Than Ever* maintains that busyness is like water to fish, the context in which life is lived that is so obvious that it often passes without comment. Busyness is found everywhere and is affecting our everyday interactions. Busyness is taken for granted; not seen as problematical, it thus remains unexamined (see Darrah, Freeman, and English-Lueck 2007). Is it not yet obvious that this plan for living is not working? It is the time again to light the new fire, sit together before the firelight of warmth and human companionship, and tell the stories that matter. Gather the family and read aloud the children's book, *If the World Were a Village* (Smith 2007), actually modeling Jesus' words: "I assure you unless you change and become like little children you will not enter the kingdom of God" (Matthew 18:3). This storybook is about world-mindedness and explores the six billion people who inhabit the planet imaging what the whole world looks like as a single global village of one hundred people. The childlike language helps the adult stewards of the world deal with some of the challenging, even frightening data. Gather friends and neighbors and watch. *An Inconvenient Truth* (2006), the film that won two Oscars at the 2007 Academy Awards and former Vice President Al Gore the 2007 Nobel Peace Prize.

We face a true planetary emergency.
The climate crisis is not a political issue,
it is a moral and spiritual challenge to all of humanity."

—Al Gore, on receiving the 2007 Nobel Peace Prize

Don't presume everyone has already seen it or that those with whom you live and work are truly aware that we have, as Gore says, entered a profoundly new period of consequences. Roger Ebert's June 2, 2006, film review is quite compelling:

> In 39 years, I have never written these words in a movie review,
> but here they are: You owe it to yourself to see this film. If

you do not, and you have grandchildren, you should explain to them why you decided not to. Am I acting as an advocate in this review? Yes, I am. I believe that to be "impartial" and "balanced" on global warming means one must take a position like Gore's. There is no other view that can be defended.

Subscribe to Chittisters's "Monastic Way," a monthly publication with daily reflections to help you walk through life whole and holy (visit www.benetvision.org). Find the courage to join the annual international creative resistance TV Turn-Off Week and experience the all but lost art of unscripted conversation. Take time to read and to talk with others about unmasking the denials and destructiveness impeding optimal living in an ecologically thriving culture and society so many are envisioning today. Subscribe online to "Vital Signs" or "State of the World," from the Worldwatch Institute, an independent research organization known around the world for its accessible, fact-based analysis of critical global issues.[5] Do something to shake yourself out of slumber.

Remaining unconscious of the
dragon's presence [lure to destructive grandiosity]
would insure that we spend most of our waking hours
experiencing what Paul Tillich called "existential estrangement"
from our best, optimal potential selves . . .
The starkness of this choice has a terrible simplicity:
you can either become conscious or stay unconscious
of the reality and presence of the dragon.
This great turn from being asleep at the wheel
to an alert knowing of the powerful proximity
of the great Other is the most important gnosis
you can ever possess about your personal, social
or spiritual life.

—Robert L. Moore, *Facing the Dragon:
Confronting Personal and Spiritual Grandiosity*

Choosing to remain in unconsciousness about what is happening within and about us will only deepen, in Tillich's words, our existential estrangement from the green sap waiting to be "sucked up" from the deep within to overflow into our nearly hardened world. The danger we fear in looking together at these cultural trends and current crises is that they will overwhelm and depress us; on the other hand, the consequences of refusing to take ownership can ultimately exact a far greater cost upon our children's children.

The question posed decades ago to Jung, Will civilization survive? has an answer:

> Enter by the narrow gate. The gate is wide and the road easy that leads to destruction and many choose to travel it. Narrow is the gate and difficult the road that leads to life, and few find it. (Matthew 7:13–14)

Roadmaps do exist. There are alternative life-ways in which to wander. People of the Book know that the wilderness wandering holds the promise of pillars of cloud by day and fire by night to guide us. We are uncomfortably summoned to the narrow gate where Spiritual Presence awaits our communal arrival. Of this we can be sure.[6]

Our global crisis is, at its root, a crisis of consciousness. Global warming, the destruction of the rainforests, the wide-scale extinction of species, acid rain, soil erosion, the depletion of the ozone layer, pollution, toxic waste, atomic waste, the energy crisis, the North-South crisis, the economic crisis, the food crisis, the water crisis, the housing crisis, the sanitation crisis, and the many other crises that humanity faces are all symptoms of a deeper psychological crisis.

The writing is on the wall. If we are to navigate our way safely through these critical times, we have to mature inwardly. Why do we feel so insecure? Why do we want to feel we are in control of things? We must discover how to move beyond this egocentric phase in our development. And fast.

—Peter Russell, *Waking Up in Time: Finding Inner Peace in Times of Accelerating Change*

Notes

1. I thank Patricia Bombard, B.V.M, D.Min., for her assistance in sharpening insights on ecofeminist spirituality as a paradigm for transformation.

2. The substance of this section is derived from the insights offered by Dr. Victoria Sweet, University of California at San Francisco, for her presentation "*Viriditas*, The Green Humor," given at Bridges to Infinity: 25th Anniversary Celebration of the International Society of the Hildegard von Bingen Studies Conference, May 30, 2008, Chestnut Hill College, Philadelphia, Pennsylvania.

3. This volume of Jung's *Collected Works* includes psychological and symbolic approaches to the Trinity and the Mass, as well as his controversial *Answer to Job*, psychological commentaries on *The Tibetan Book of the Great Liberation* and *The Tibetan Book of the Dead*, "Yoga and the West," and "The Psychology of Eastern Meditation."

4. Jung's use of "green" or "greenness" appears twenty times in the index to Jung's *Collected Works*.

5. Worldwatch Institute, 1776 Massachusetts Avenue, NW Washington, DC 20036, www.worldwatch.org.

6. Some insights in this chapter have previously appeared in "Into This Dark Night: Disquieting Hopeful Reflections," *New Theology Review*, vol. 19, no. 3 (Collegeville, Minn.: Liturgical Press, August 2006), 62–71.

Application

Get a sense of life in our present time from a global perspective by logging onto Peter Russell's world clock and click the button that says "Now" (Peterrussell.dreamhosters.com/Odds/World Clock.php).

In real time, you can watch the world's population increase as people are born and die. You can see how many acres of forests are being cut down and how many being replanted. You can see how many dollars are being spent on the military; how many species have gone extinct. Absorb as much as you can and then turn off the computer and sit quietly. Then consider:

What did I experience?

What is my response to the information?

What does it matter?

What is it like to wake up?

What will I do next?

Epilogue

Headstrong and humble,
annoying and comforting,
Hildegard was real.

> —Carmen Acevedo Butcher,
> *Hildegard of Bingen: A Spiritual Reader*

He was not a saint.
In fact, many accounts of his behavior and attitudes
indicate shortness of temper, irascibility,
bluntness to the point of brutality,
impiety and skepticism . . .
He was not a faithful husband
nor a very conscientious father.
He was a man who could be himself completely,
blemishes and all.

> —Murray Stein on Jung, *Jung's Treatment of*
> *Christianity*

The irrational fulness of life has taught me
never to discard anything, even when it goes
against all our theories (so short-lived at best)
or otherwise admits of no immediate explanation.
It is of course disquieting, and one is not certain
whether the compass is pointing true or not;
but security, certitude, and peace
do not lead to discoveries.

> —C. G. Jung, from "Foreword to the *I Ching*"

Long ago God lived in the tabernacle,
and only a priest had the key.
Not only were we locked out,
but God was locked in.
There was safety in this arrangement.
Then, somehow, the box became broken
in the twentieth century, and God got out.
Very few of us seem to know
what to do with this desperate fact:
God is loose!
God is out and is now appearing everywhere.
I would love to read a history book
written a hundred years in the future
to see what we will do with the new power.
It has wonderful possibilities and
dreadful consequences if it goes wrong.
>   —Robert A. Johnson, *Balancing Heaven and Earth*

So what?

Not too many years ago, I was asked by a province of Franciscan friars to prepare and deliver a presentation on what the Spirit might be doing today in the midst of our turbulent and uncertain times. I spent months reading and preparing a thoughtful, well-researched, and artistic presentation, which I delivered to a hundred or so friars. The next morning, a young Franciscan emerged from the audience, went to the microphone, and said he had been thinking about what to say in response to my presentation and what kept running through his head was "So what?" My initial surprise mixed with distress quickly turned as he smiled and proceeded to explain. He said it is the question he asks himself after he reads the homily he intends to preach on Sunday. It is the question he asks himself whenever he is faced with what he perceives to be a confrontation. "So what? What is going on here that has to do with what really matters?" I found myself asking this question when I reread all of what I have written here in *Experiencing Hildegard*. So what? Keep that question in mind.

Both twelfth-century Benedictine Abbess Hildegard of Bingen and twentieth-century pioneer of modern depth psychology Carl Jung sought to heal a Christianity in crisis. Both believed that the personal and communal, the individual and collective were connected at the D/depth. Each experienced a visionary life that gripped them from within with images and ideas that have survived beyond their own lives. One was an actual, literal, and historical monastic; the other carried the monk within. In addition, in all honesty, both were elitists. Hildegard accepted only well-dowried women of nobility into her monastery, eschewing those of lesser birth. Jung lived a privileged life as an educated European male with all the accompanying prerogatives, including involvement with another woman who was not his wife and having the luxury of time all to himself, all about himself. While truly persons drenched in the assumptions of their times, they also transcended their personal lives and freed their thinking and feeling beyond the confines of their cultures and their particular eras. They each lived into their eighties with little pretense in them, ever. Thus, a medieval woman and a modern man offer a glimpse into our own capacity to do the same by presenting a whole life for our deep consideration of the present we desire to live and the future we choose to help bring about. We are called to cultivate the inner nun and monk, especially in the time that is ours. The journey traverses metaphorical and spiritual hills and valleys from which no one is exempt. It cannot be said more clearly than Jung did in a letter from 1923:

> I consider it my task and duty to educate my patients and pupils to the point where they can accept the direct demand that is made upon them from within. This path is so difficult that I cannot see how the indispensable sufferings along the way could be supplanted by any kind of technical procedure. Through my study of the early Christian writings I have gained a deep and indelible impression of how dreadfully serious an experience of God is. It will be no different today. (*Letters* 1, p. 41)

Hildegard's tenacity of spirit is a testimony to the fruit of inner suffering that accompanies encounter with the *Mysterium*. In a letter she wrote in 1175 at the age of 70, she says that through the inner journey "all is transformed and all sorrow and tribulation is consigned to oblivion" (*Letters,* vol. 2, p. 24). All self-absorbing pain and debilitation evaporated when she faced her fears and resistance to the burning message within. Her own *Vita* records that she was afflicted until she could name the place from which she was living. Her openness to the unconscious is stunning. Therein is the decision to know God who is consuming fire and still small voice.

> The perpetual hesitation of the
> neurotic to launch out into life is
> readily explained by his desire to stand
> aside so as not to get involved in the
> dangerous struggle for existence. But
> anyone who refuses to experience
> life must stifle his desire to live—in other
> words, he must commit partial suicide.
>
> —C. G. Jung, *Symbols of Transformation*, par. 165

As visitants from the past carrying messages with future content, Hildegard and Jung addressed with unhesitating directness the consequences of neglecting or repressing our innate introspective, critically self-reflective capacities and abilities. They both foresaw and forewarned that the outcomes of the apparent successes in conquering nature subdued our own wildness in such a way as to alienate ourselves from the dark unconscious, the dark cloud where God is (Exodus 20:21). A healthy dose of fear of the Lord and trust in the One who beckons us to the deep waters and leads us to life and life in abundance are needed for this journey. And it begins where we are living right now.

The preceding reflection is a preface to answering the question posed earlier: "So what? So what now? What really matters?" If you are serious about *experiencing* the spiritual journey, then the desire for God must be authentic and dauntless. It is primarily a deeply personal decision with tremendous social consequences. But, the spiritual adventure begins first within. As Jung said,

The great events of world history are, at bottom, profoundly unimportant. In the last analysis, the essential thing is the life of the individual. This alone makes history. Here alone do the great transformations first take place, and the whole future, the whole history of the world, ultimately spring as a gigantic summation from these hidden sources in individuals. In our most private and subjective lives we are not only passive witnesses of our age, and its sufferers, but also its makers. We make our own epoch. (C. G. Jung Institute 1983)

How and will we make the epoch that is the time that is uniquely ours on earth? We are not responsible for all the ills that have and will befall us, but since we inhabit this earth, this world, this country, our neighborhood, institutions, and family, it is—all of it—our home. We are responsible for the home we may not have created but in which we live and move and have our being (Acts 17:28). So what is the condition of your inner world and its workings? So how is your living contributing to the transformation of our postmodern, fragmented, unprecedented, turbocharged life riddled with more tribulations than can be named?

In 1961, the last year of his life, Jung was asked how long the transformation of Christianity would take. "About six hundred years," Jung conjectured. "Where do you know this from?" he was asked in reply, and he responded, "From dreams. From other people's and my own. This new religion will come together as far as we can see" (Stein 1985, p. 188). It does not seem that Jung foresaw so much an emerging new religion as an evolved and healed Christianity. Jungian theologian John Dourley, however, wonders if Jung actually meant something more. Would a new religious consciousness do the same thing for Christianity that Christianity did for Judaism? Is Christianity actually outgrowing itself in ways that would make its future as different from its present as Christianity ultimately became from Judaism? Such a new religious consciousness is far more extensive and profound than a renewal or evolution of Christianity. Will it one day be possible to speak of "natural grace" or the "grace of nature" when deeply embedded dualism is finally and fully overcome? Only time will reveal.

Six hundred years from 1961 is the year 2561. This is five hundred and fifty-two years from now. We are, as the universe itself, work-in-progress. As Jung said in a letter of condolence, "Life, so-called, is a short episode between two great mysteries, which yet are one" (1984, p. 77). In the short episode of our individual lives, rich with mystery, misery, and magnificence, the potentiality exits for each of us to realize a wise old woman like Hildegard and a wise old man like Jung alive within us.

Her work shows us that, within us,
the Incarnation lives,
Spring greens,
Light shines,
Music sings,
Bread sustains,
Words instruct, and—
Even though dark, avaricious wolves prowl—
Stars are bright and Love heals.

—Carmen Acevedo Butcher, *Hildegard of Bingen: A Spiritual Reader*

No matter what the world thinks about religious experience,
the one who has it possesses a great treasure,
a thing that has become for him a source of life,
meaning, and beauty, and that has given a new splendour
to the world and to mankind.
He has *pistis* [faith] and peace.

—C. G. Jung, "Psychology and Religion," par. 167

Therefore anyone who wants to know the human psyche. . . .
would be better advised to . . . bid farewell to his study, and
wander with human heart through the world. There,
in the horrors of prisons, lunatic asylums and hospitals,
in drab suburban pubs, in brothels and gambling-hells,
in the salons of the elegant, the Stock Exchanges,
Socialist meetings, churches, revivalist gatherings and
ecstatic sects, through love and hate, through the
experience of passion in every form in his own body,
he would reap richer stores of knowledge than
text-books a foot thick could give him, and
he will know how to doctor the sick with
real knowledge of the human soul.

—C. G. Jung, "New Paths in Psychology," par. 409

Seven References
to Hildegard of Bingen
in Jung's Collected Works

The following provides the specific references to Hildegard of Bingen in Jung's *Collected Works*. They have been ordered according to the volume number in which they appear. For each citation, a brief overview of the context in which Jung was working situates his use of Hildegard for the reader.

1. *Symbols of Transformation* (1952), *CW,* vol. 5 (Princeton, N.J.: Princeton University Press, 1967), pars. 138–139.

This work is concerned with the importance of living with and in a myth. Jung asks the question: "What is the myth you are living?" (p. xxiv) and then responds, "The real purpose of this book is confined to working out the implications of all those historical and spiritual factors which come together in the involuntary products of individual fantasy" (p. xxix). In short, Jung is investigating subjective contents as the products of unconscious processes via "The Miller Fantasies," a case study of a young American woman using the pseudonym Frank Miller. Reference to Hildegard appears in Part III of *Symbols of Transformation*, "The Miller Fantasies: Anamnesis." In section V, "The Song of the Moth," Jung says:

> In mysticism the inwardly perceived vision of the Divine is often nothing but sun or light, and is rarely, if ever, personified. . . . Hildegard of Bingen (1100–1178) declares:
>
> > But the light I see is not local, but is everywhere, and brighter far than the cloud which supports the sun. I can in no way know the form of this light, just as I cannot see the sun's disc entire. But in this light I see at times, though not often, another light which is called by me the living light, but when and in what manner I see this I do not know how to say. And when I see it all weariness and need is lifted from me, and all at once I feel like a simple girl and not like an old woman.

I thank John Dourley who, five years ago, first assisted me in locating these references. John Dourley is Professor Emeritus, Department of Religion, at Carleton University, Ottawa, Canada. He graduated as a Jungian analyst from the Zürich/Küsnacht Institute and has published widely on Jung and religion.

ng cites the source for Hildegard's commentary on her visionary exper-
ence in footnote 26, which reads: "In Pitra, *Analecta sacra*, VIII, p. 333."
The full text of the excerpt can be found in Hildegard's letter to Guibert of
Gembloux available in *The Personal Correspondence of Hildegard of Bingen:
Selected Letters with Introduction and Commentary*, Joseph L. Baird, ed. (New
York: Oxford University Press, 2006), pp. 136–42.

2. "Concerning Mandala Symbolism" (1950), in *CW*, vol. 9i, *The Archetypes
and the Collective Unconscious* (Princeton, N.J.: Princeton University Press,
1968), par. 703, figure 48.

This book gives the nucleus of Jung's work on the theory and meaning
of archetypes in relation to the psyche as a whole. In "Concerning Mandala
Symbolism," Jung explores the meaning of the mandala, a Sanskrit word
meaning "circle." He provides visual images of mandalas in the text that
include images from India, Egypt, the ancient Tibetan Wheel, a Gothic
window in the cathedral at Paderborn, a Roman mosaic, and the Navaho
Indians, but most of the fifty-four illustrations are done by his patients,
young and old, male and female. Jung says,

> There are innumerable variants of the motif shown here, but
> they all are based on the squaring of a circle. Their basic motif
> is the premonition of a centre of personality, a kind of central
> point within the psyche, to which everything is related, by which
> everything is arranged, and which is itself a source of energy.
> The energy of the central point is manifested in the almost
> irresistible compulsion and urge to *become what one is* . . . .
> (par. 634)

Jung includes a Hildegardian mandala in figure 48, which is from the
Lucca manuscript of the *Book of Divine Works*, Vision 4. Jung says, "This
picture, from a manuscript of Hildegard of Bingen, shows the earth
surrounded by the ocean, realm of air, and starry heaven. The actual globe
of the earth in the centre is divided into four" (par. 703).

Jung identifies the transcultural function of mandalas as instruments
of meditation, symbolizations of individuation and integration, and
realizations of the inner experience. He says, "They express the idea of a
safe refuge, of inner reconciliation and wholeness" (par. 710). Jung notes
he could have produced many more pictures from all parts of the world,
but what would be true of all—as of the fifty-four images included—is
that the same or very similar symbols are produced at all times, in all
places, and among people of enormous diversity. Transconsciousness is
born through the collective unconscious. Hildegard creates a mandala with
no conscious awareness of its existence in Tibetan Buddhism or Dervish
monasteries. This is the action of the archetypes. Of this Jung says, "And
when we penetrate a little more deeply below the surface of the psyche,

we come upon historical layers which are not just dead dust, but alive and continuously active in everyone—maybe to a degree that we cannot imagine in the present state of our knowledge" (par. 712).

3. "Flying Saucers: A Modern Myth of Things Seen in the Skies," (1958), in *CW,* vol. 10, *Civilization in Transition* (Princeton, N.J.: Princeton University Press, 1964), pars. 765–769, plate VIII.

Volume 10 includes, among other topics, a 1918 essay, "The Role of the Unconscious," on the modern discovery of the unconscious, importance of self-knowledge in dealing with social pressures, relations between the sexes, and ethnic factors in psychological theory. In "Flying Saucers: A Modern Myth of Things Seen in the Skies," Jung is interpreting the reports of unexplained lights in the sky as a psychological phenomenon. Jung uses one of Hildegard's illuminations from the *Scivias,* "The Quickening of the Child in the Womb," which illustrates the four-sided Trinity and abundant "remarkable symbolism." For the larger context for Jung's inclusion of Hildegard, see pp. 383–412, especially pp. 403–6, pars. 765–69, for specific reference to Jung's interpretation of Hildegard's illumination, which appears in plate 8 of this volume.

4. "Psychology and Religion" (1940), in *CW,* vol. 11, *Psychology and Religion* (Princeton, N.J.: Princeton University Press, 1969), par. 151.

Jung provides a wide definition of religion: Religion, he says, is "a careful and scrupulous observation of what Rudolf Otto aptly termed the *numinosum*" (p. v). Jung says that he is not addressing his remarks to people who possess Christian faith, "but to those many people for whom the light has gone out, the mystery has faded, and God is dead" (par. 148). Jung explores key aspects of Western religion in Part I and Eastern religion in Part II. This is the volume that includes psychological and symbolic approaches to the Trinity and the Mass, as well as his controversial, "Answer to Job." Jung writes psychological commentaries on *The Tibetan Book of the Great Liberation* and *The Tibetan Book of the Dead* and essays on yoga and the West and the psychology of Eastern meditation.

Jung considers ancient texts that refer to the spirit found in natural phenomenon. He says,

> This spirit, coming from God, is also the cause of the "greenness," the *benedicta viriditas,* much praised by the alchemists. Mylius [JD Mylius, seventeenth-century philosopher and alchemical book engraver] says of it: "God has breathed into created things . . . a kind of germination, which is the viridescence." In Hildegard of Bingen's Hymn to the Holy Ghost, which begins "O ignis Spiritus paraclite," we read: "From you the clouds rain down, the heavens move, the stones have their moisture, the waters give forth streams, and the earth sweats out greenness." (par. 151)

5. "Commentary on 'The Secret of the Golden Flower'" (1957), in *CW,* vol. 13, *Alchemical Studies* (Princeton, N.J.: Princeton University Press, 1967), pars. 42–44.

The editorial note that accompanies this essay comments on its historical importance. In *Memories, Dreams, Reflections* (chapter 7), Jung comments that the nature of alchemy became of true importance to him only after reading the ancient Chinese text of "The Secret of the Golden Flower," sent to him in 1928 by Richard Wilhelm. By 1939, Jung's thinking matured to include the conviction that medieval alchemy provided the long-sought connecting link between Gnosis and the processes of the collective unconscious that can be observed in the modern personality (p. 4).

In his "Commentary on 'The Secret of the Golden Flower,'" Jung deals with the challenges of the Western mind to grasp the concepts of Eastern thought. He speaks of Hildegard and explores the phenomenon of inner spiritual experience:

> The phenomenon itself, the vision of light, is an experience common to many mystics, and one that is undoubtedly of the greatest significance, because at all times and places it proves to be something unconditioned and absolute, a combination of supreme power and profound meaning. Hildegard of Bingen, an outstanding personality quite apart from her mysticism, writes in much the same way about her central vision:
>
>> Since my childhood I have always seen a light in my soul, but not with the outer eyes, nor through the thoughts of my heart; neither do the five outer senses take part in this vision. . . . The light I perceive is not of a local kind, but is much brighter than the cloud which supports the sun. I cannot distinguish height, breadth, or length in it. . . . What I see or learn in such a vision stays long in my memory. I see, hear, and know in the same moment. . . . I cannot recognize any sort of form in this light, although I sometimes see in it another light that is known to me as the living light. . . . While I am enjoying the spectacle of this light, all sadness and sorrow vanish from my memory.
>
> I myself know a few individuals who have had personal experience of this phenomenon. So far as I have been able to understand it, it seems to have to do with an acute state of consciousness, as intense as it is abstract, a "detached" consciousness, which, as Hildegard implies, brings into awareness areas of psychic happenings ordinarily covered in darkness. . . . As a rule the phenomenon is spontaneous, coming and going on its own initiative. Its effect is astonishing in that it almost always brings

about a solution of psychic complications and frees the inner personality from emotional and intellectual entanglements, thus creating a unity of being which is universally felt as "liberation." (pars. 42–43)

6. *Mysterium Coniunctionis* (1955–1956), *CW,* vol. 14 (Princeton, N.J.: Princeton University Press, 1970), footnote 173.

Volume 14 of the *Collected Works* presents Jung's last great work, in which he was engaged for more than a decade, from 1941 to 1954. He finished it in his eightieth year. The book gives a final account of his lengthy research into the symbolic significance of alchemy for modern depth psychology. In section VI, "On the Conjunction," Jung discusses the symbolism of water and water-bearers, such as clouds and dew, and how these images are found in many kinds of ancient texts. It is in this context that a reference to Hildegard appears in a lengthy footnote in which Jung makes reference to the following comment by Hildegard: "'From thee the clouds flow,' says Hildegard of Bingen of the Holy Ghost" (par. 727, footnote 173). Images of clouds, rain, and dew—water sources—are spiritually rich images. Jung cites a liturgical prayer from the Roman Missal—the Introit from the fourth Sunday of Advent—"Drop down dew, ye heavens, from above, and let the clouds rain down the Just One: let the earth open and bud forth a Saviour" (ibid.).

7. "The Hypothesis of the Collective Unconscious" (1932), in *CW,* vol. 18, *The Symbolic Life: Miscellaneous Writings* (Princeton, N.J.: Princeton University Press, 1976), par. 1225.

This final volume of the *Collected Works* provides an ample collection of miscellany that includes one hundred and thirty assorted writings: lectures, short essays, forewords to books, correspondence, all covering a wide range of topics spanning a timeframe from 1901 until Jung's death in 1961.

In "The Hypothesis of the Collective Unconscious," a brief abstract of a lecture delivered in Zürich in 1932, Jung indicates that the lecture will demonstrate the mandala symbolism and the parallelism between the symbol of the circle as produced by his educated patients in treatment and the ritual mandalas from a variety of times and cultures, including the visions of Hildegard of Bingen. The modern pictures Jung presented were derived from people who produced their mandalas spontaneously without the influence of knowledge of ancient mandala ritual and symbolism. In the précis of this lecture, Jung notes he will be using "the visions of Hildegard of Bingen from the Codex Lucca (12th to 13th cent.)" The manuscript of the lecture has not been found.

A Brief Chronology of Hildegard's Life

1095	First Crusade
1098	Hildegard's birth at Bermersheim near Alzey in Rheinhessen. She is the tenth and last child of Hildebert of Bermersheim and his wife Mechthild.
1099	Crusaders capture Jerusalem, wresting it from Muslim control.
1106	Hildegard enters an enclosure with Jutta of Spanheim that is attached to the recently founded Benedictine monastery of Disibodenberg. Jutta becomes her teacher.
1112–1115	Hildegard takes her vows and receives the veil as a Benedictine nun from Bishop Otto of Bamberg. The enclosure grows and becomes a convent.
1136	Death of Jutta of Spanheim. The nuns elect Hildegard as their leader.
1141	Hildegard begins to write *Scivias*, her first major theological work. Her friend, the monk Volmar, and the nun Richardis von Stade act as her secretaries.
1146–1148	Hildegard exchanges letters with Bernard of Clairvaux.
1147–1148	Pope Eugenius III reads from *Scivias* at the Synod of Trier. He authorizes Hildegard to continue her work. Hildegard begins to correspond with many distinguished people. Hildegard is inspired by God to move from Disibodenberg to Rupertsburg, which she successfully initiates against the wishes of the monks.
1147–1149	Second Crusade
1148	A letter from Master Odo of Paris reveals that Hildegard's songs are already well known.
1150	Having lived at Disibodenberg for forty-four years, Hildegard moves to Rupertsburg with some eighteen or twenty nuns.

1151–1158	Composition of the *Natural History* and *Causes and Cures,* the only two medical texts known to have been composed in the medieval era.
1151	Hildegard finishes *Scivias.* Richardis accepts election as abbess of a convent at Bassum, near Bremen, against Hildegard's wishes.
1152	Frederick I (Barbarossa) is elected King. Hildegard writes him a letter in tribute. Richardis dies.
After 1154	Hildegard meets Frederick I at Ingelheim.
1155	Hildegard persuades the monks of Disibodenberg to relinquish the lands given as part of the nuns' dowry.
1158–1161	Hildegard falls ill. At age sixty, she undertakes her first preaching tour, which takes her along the River Main as far as Bamberg.
1158–1163	Composition of the *Book of Life's Merits.* This period marks the beginning of the eighteen-year-long schism between the papacy and Frederick I. The first antipope is Victor IV.
1160	Hildegard's second preaching tour. She preaches publicly in Trier, then proceeds by way of Metz and Krauftal to Hördt.
1161–1163	Hildegard's third preaching tour, following the Rhine northward to Cologne, and then on to Werden.
1163	Now sixty-five, she begins to write the *Book of Divine Works.* She writes again to Frederick I and appears to adopt a neutral position in the schism. She receives an edict of imperial protection in perpetuity for Rupertsburg.
1164	The second antipope, Paschal III, comes to power. Hildegard writes for a third time to Frederick, this time adopting a critical tone.
Around 1165	At sixty-seven, fifteen years after founding Rupertsburg, Hildegard founds the community at Eibingen, overlooking Rudesheim, on the east bank on the Rhine, which she visits twice a week. She writes to Henry II of England and to his wife, Queen Eleanor.
1167–1170	Hildegard falls ill again.
1168	The third antipope, Callistus III, is consecrated. Hildegard writes to Frederick I, warning him of divine judgment.

1169	Hildegard heals (performs an exorcism upon) the possessed woman, Sigewize, and receives her into her community at Rupertsburg.
1170	Composition of *The Life of St. Disibod*, at the request of Abbot Helenger of Disibodenberg.
1170–1171	Hildegard's fourth preaching tour, at age seventy-two, takes her south to Zwiefalten.
1173	Volmar dies after forty years as Hildegard's secretary.
1173–1174	Hildegard completes the *Book of Divine Works*. A conflict arises regarding the appointment of Volmar's successor.
1174–1175	The monk Gottfried arrives from Disibodenberg. He begins to write the *Life of Hildegard* and completes Book One.
1175	Guibert of Gembloux begins a correspondence with Hildegard. She sends him her *Book of Life's Merits* and her *Songs*.
1176	Gottfried dies.
1177	Guibert of Gembloux becomes Hildegard's secretary.
1178	An interdict is imposed on the Rupertsburg monastery by the diocese of Mainz. The nuns are prohibited from sung praise and communion for having buried an "excommunicated" man.
1179	The interdict is lifted by Archbishop Christian of Mainz. Hildegard dies on September 17 at age eighty-one.
1180–1190	Theodoric of Echternach completes Books Two and Three of the *Life of Hildegard*.
1227	Canonization proceedings begin forty-eight years after her death. By the sixteenth century, Hildegard appears in *The Roman Martyrology* of Baronius. Sainthood remains controversial.
1916	Hildegard's feast day, September 17, is awarded the official rank of *memoria*—the lowest degree of memorial celebration.
1940	September 17 is added to the German Feast Day calendar.
1979	German bishops petition Rome to have Hildegard declared a Doctor of the Church (to join Teresa of Avila and Catherine of Siena).

1997   One hundred years after her death, Therese of Lisieux
                  ("The Little Flower") is declared the third female Doctor
                  of the Church by Pope John Paul II.

Bibliography

Works by Hildegard of Bingen

Works by Hildegard are cited in the text by title, with dates where there are multiple editions.

The Book of Divine Works (with Letters and Songs). Matthew Fox, ed. Santa Fe: Bear and Company, 1987.

Book of the Rewards of Life. Bruce Hozeski, trans. New York: Oxford University Press, 1997.

Explanation of the Rule of Benedict. Hugh Feiss, trans. Toronto: Peregrina, 1990.

Hildegard of Bingen: Mystical Writings. Fiona Bowie and Oliver Davies, eds. New York: Crossroad, 1995.

Hildegard of Bingen: Selected Writings. Mark Atherton, trans. New York: Penguin Books, 2001.

Hildegard's Healing Plants: From Her Medieval Classic Physica. Bruce Hozeski, trans. Boston: Beacon Press, 2001.

Hildegard von Bingen's Physica: *The Complete English Translation of Her Classic Work on Health and Healing*. Priscilla Throop, trans. Rochester, Vt.: Healing Arts Press, 1998.

Hildegard von Bingen's Mystical Visions. Bruce Hozeski, trans. Santa Fe: Bear and Company, 1986.

Illuminations of Hildegard of Bingen. Matthew Fox, ed. Santa Fe: Bear and Company, 1985.

The Letters of Hildegard of Bingen. 3 vols. Joseph L. Baird and Radd K. Ehrman, trans. New York: Oxford University Press, 1994, 1998, and 2004.

On Natural Philosophy and Medicine: Selections from Cause et cure. Margret Berger, ed. and trans. Cambridge: D. S. Brewer, 1999.

Physica. Priscilla Throop, trans. Rochester, Vt.: Healing Arts Press, 1998.

Scivias. Bruce Hozeski, trans. Santa Fe: Bear and Company, 1986.

Scivias. Mother Columba Hart and Jane Bishop, trans. New York: Paulist Press, 1990.

Secrets of God: Writings of Hildegard of Bingen. Sheila Flanagan, trans. Boston: Shambhala, 1996.

Symphonia: A Critical Edition of the Symphonia Armonie Celestium Revelationum (Symphony of the Harmony of Celestial Revelations). 2nd revised edition. Barbara Newman, ed. and trans. Ithaca, N.Y.: Cornell University Press.

References

Alcoholics Anonymous. 1939. *The Big Book*. New York: Author.

Adams, Carol J., ed. 1994. *Ecofeminism and the Sacred*. New York: Continuum International Publishing Group.

Allen, Prudence. 1987. Two medieval views on women's identity: Hildegard of Bingen and Thomas Aquinas. *Studies in Religion* 16(1):21–36.

———. 1989. Hildegard of Bingen's philosophy of sex identity. *Thought* 64:231–41.

Baldwin, Christina. 1990. *Life's Companion: Journal Writing as a Spiritual Quest*. New York: Bantam.

Beer, Frances. 1992. *Women and Mystical Experience in the Middle Ages*. Rochester, N.Y.: Boydell.

Berman, Morris. 2000. "The Monastic Option in the Twenty-First Century." In *The Twilight of American Culture*. New York: W. W. Norton and Company.

Berry, Thomas. 1991. *Befriending the Earth: A Theology of Reconciliation Between Humans and the Earth*. Mystic, Conn.: Twenty-Third Publications.

Browning, Elizabeth Barrett. 1897. *Aurora Leigh and Other Poems*. New York: Oxford University Press, 2008.

Burnett, Charles, and Peter Dronke, eds. 1998. *Hildegard of Bingen: The Context of Her Thought and Art*. London: Warburg Institute.

Butcher, Carmen Acevedo. 2007. *Hildegard of Bingen: A Spiritual Reader*. Brewster, Mass.: Paraclete Press.

———. 2008. "Hildegard of Bingen and Her Love of the Polysemous Logos." Presentation given at "Bridges to Infinity": 25th Anniversary Celebration of the International Society of the Hildegard von Bingen Studies Conference, May 30, Chestnut Hill College, Philadelphia, Penn.

Bynum, Caroline Walker. 1979. *Docere Verbo et Exemplo: An Aspect of Twelfth Century Spirituality*. Missoula, Mont.: Edward Brothers, Inc.

———. 1982. *Jesus as Mother: Studies in Spirituality of the High Middle Ages*. Berkeley: University of California Press.

———. 1987. *Holy Feast and Holy Fast: The Religious Significance of Food to Medieval Women*. Berkeley: University of California Press.

———. 1992. *Fragmentation and Redemption: Essays on Gender and the Human Body in Medieval Religion*. New York: Zone Books.

Bynum, Caroline Walker, Steve Harrell, and Paula Richman, eds. 1985. *Gender and Religion: The Complexity of Symbols*. Boston: Beacon Press.

C. G. Jung Institute. 1983. "Matter of Heart: The Extraordinary Journey of C.G. Jung into the Soul of Man." DVD. Los Angeles: The C.G. Jung Institute.

Cantor, Norman F. 1994. *Medieval Lives: Eight Charismatic Men and Women of the Middle Ages*. New York: HarperCollins.

Carr, Anne. 1988. *Transforming Grace*. San Francisco: Harper and Row, 1988.

Cherewatuk, Karen, and Ulrike Wiethaus, eds. 1993. *Dear Sister: Medieval Women and the Epistolary Genre*. Philadelphia: University of Pennsylvania Press.

Chittister, Joan. 2008. *The Gift of Years*. New York: BlueBridge.

Churchill, Laurie J., Phyllis R. Brown, and Jane E. Jeffrey, eds. 2002. *Women Writing Latin*. 3 vols. London: Routledge.

Clark, Elizabeth. 1983. *Women in the Early Church*. Wilmington, Del.: Michael Glazier.

Craine, Renate. 1997. *Hildegard: Prophet of the Cosmic Christ*. New York: Crossroad.

D'Arcens, Louise, and Juanita Feros Ruys, eds. 2004. *Maistresse of My Wit: Medieval Women, Modern Scholars. Making the Middle Ages*, vol. 7. Turnout, Belgium: Brepols Publishers.

Daly, Mary. 1978. *Gyn/Ecology: The Metaethics of Radical Feminism*. Boston: Beacon Press.

Darrah, Charles N., James M. Freeman, and J. A. English-Lueck. 2007. *Busier Than Ever! Why American Families Can't Slow Down*. Stanford, Calif.: Stanford University Press.

de Hemptinne, Thérèse, and Maria Eugenia Gongora, eds. 2004. *The Voice of Silence: Women's Literacy in a Men's Church. Medieval Church Studies*, vol. 9. Turnout, Belgium: Brepols Publishers.

Doniger, Wendy. 1999. *Splitting the Difference*. Chicago: University of Chicago Press.

Dreyer, Elizabeth. 2005. *Passionate Spirituality: Hildegard of Bingen and Hadewijch of Brabant*. New York: Paulist Press.

Dreyer, Elizabeth, and Mark S. Burrows. 2005. *Minding the Spirit: The Study of Christian Spirituality*. Baltimore: The John Hopkins University Press.

Dronke, Peter. 1984. *Women Writers of the Middle Ages: A Critical Study of Texts from Perpetua (203) to Marguerite Porete (1310)*. Cambridge, Mass.: Cambridge University Press.

Dronke, Peter, ed. and trans. 1994. *Nine Medieval Latin Plays*. Cambridge, Mass.: Cambridge University Press.

Farmer, Sharon, and Carol Braun Pasternack, eds. 2003. *Gender and Difference in the Middle Ages*. Minneapolis: University of Minnesota Press.

Fierro, Nancy. 1994. *Hildegard of Bingen and Her Vision of the Feminine*. Lanham, Md.: Sheed and Ward.

Flanagan, Sabina. 1989 *Hildegard of Bingen, 1098–1179: A Visionary Life*. New York: Routledge.

———. 1995. Hildegard von Bingen (1098–1179). Retrieved January 27, 2009, from http://www.hildegard.org/documents/flanagan.html# meritorum

Ford-Grabowsky, Mary. 1985. *The Concept of Christian Faith in the Light of Hildegard of Bingen and C. G. Jung: A Critical Alternative to Fowler.* Ph.D. diss., Princeton Theological Seminary.

Fournier-Rosset, Jany. 1999. *From Saint Hildegard's Kitchen: Foods of Health, Foods of Joy.* Ligouri, Mo.: Ligouri Publications.

Garry, Ann, and Marilyn Pearsall. 1989. *Women, Knowledge and Reality: Explorations in Feminist Philosophy.* Boston: Unwin Hyman.

Gies, Frances, and Joseph Gies. 1978. *Women in the Middle Ages.* New York: Crowell.

Gossmann, Elisabeth. 1995. *Hildegard of Bingen: Four Papers.* Toronto: Peregrina.

Gottfried of Disibodenberg and Theodoric of Echternach. 1995. *The Life of the Holy Hildegard.* Adelgundis Führkötter, OSB, and James McGrath, trans. Mary Palmquist and John Kulas, OSB, eds. Collegeville, Minn.: The Liturgical Press.

———. 1996. *The Life of Saintly Hildegard.* Hugh Feiss, OSB, trans. Toronto: Peregrina.

Grant, Barbara L. 1980. Five liturgical songs by Hildegard von Bingen (1098–1179). *Signs: Journal of Women in Culture and Society* 5:557–567.

Gunn, John, and Patricia Kelly. 1999. *Hildegard: A Play.* Avalon Beach, NSW: Turnkey Productions/University of Queensland Press.

Haugen, Marty. 1980. "We Remember" (for SATB chorus, keyboard accompaniment, and 2 trumpets). Celebration Series. Chicago: GIA Publications.

Hopkins, Gerard Manley. 1952. *Poems of Gerard Manley Hopkins.* London: Oxford University Press.

Jaffé, Aniela. 1989. *Was C. G. Jung a Mystic?* Einsiedeln: Daimon Verlag.

Jaffé, Aniela, ed. 1979. *Word and Image.* Princeton, N.J.: Princeton University Press.

John, Helen J. 1992. Hildegard of Bingen: A new twelfth-century woman philosopher? *Hypatia* 7(1):115–23.

Johnson, Elizabeth. 2008. *Quest for the Living God.* New York: Continuum.

Johnson, Robert A. 1993. *Owning Your Own Shadow: Understanding the Dark Side of the Psyche.* New York: Harper One.

Jung, C. G. 1912. New paths in psychology. In *CW,* vol. 7. Princeton, N.J.: Princeton University Press, second edition, 1966.

———. 1931. The spiritual problem of modern man. In *CW,* vol. 10. Princeton, N.J.: Princeton University Press, 1964.

———. 1932a. Psychotherapists or the clergy. In *CW,* vol. 11. Princeton, N.J.: Princeton University Press, 1969.

———. 1932b. Foreword to Harding: *The Way of All Women.* In *CW,* vol. 18. Princeton, N.J.: Princeton University Press, 1976.

———. 1935. The relations between the ego and the unconscious. In *CW,* vol. 7. Princeton, N.J.: Princeton University Press, 1966.

————. 1939. What India can teach us. In *CW,* vol. 10. Princeton, N.J.: Princeton University Press, 1964.

————. 1940. Psychology and religion. In *CW,* vol. 11. Princeton, N.J.: Princeton University Press, 1969.

————. 1945. After the catastrophe. In *CW,* vol. 10. Princeton, N.J.: Princeton University Press, 1964.

————. 1948. The phenomenology of the spirit in fairytales. In *CW,* vol. 9i. Princeton, N.J.: Princeton University Press, 1968.

————. 1950a. Concerning mandala symbolism. In *CW,* vol. 9i. Princeton, N.J.: Princeton University Press, 1968.

————. 1950b. A study in the process of individuation. In *CW,* vol. 9i. Princeton, N.J.: Princeton University Press, 1968.

————. 1952a. Answer to Job. In *CW,* vol. 11. Princeton, N.J.: Princeton University Press, 1969.

————. 1952b. *Symbols of Transformation. CW,* vol. 5. Princeton, N.J.: Princeton University Press, 1967.

————. 1952c. *Psychology and Alchemy. CW,* vol. 12. Princeton, N.J.: Princeton University Press, 1968.

————. 1954a. Archetypes of the collective unconscious. In *CW,* vol. 9i. Princeton, N.J.: Princeton University Press, 1968.

————. 1954b. Psychological aspects of the mother archetype. In *CW,* vol. 9i. Princeton, N.J.: Princeton University Press, 1968.

————. 1955–56. *Mysterium Coniunctionis. CW,* vol. 14. Princeton, N.J.: Princeton University Press, 1970.

————. 1957. Commentary on "The Secret of the Golden Flower." In *CW,* vol. 13. Princeton, N.J.: Princeton University Press, 1967.

————. 1958. Flying saucers: A modern myth of things seen in the skies." In *CW,* vol. 10. Princeton, N.J.: Princeton University Press, 1964.

————. 1959. Good and evil in analytical psychology. In *CW,* vol. 10. Princeton, N.J.: Princeton University Press, 1964.

————. 1964. *Man and His Symbols.* Marie-Louise von Franz, Joseph L. Henderson, Jolande Jacobi, and Aniela Jaffé, eds. New York: Doubleday.

————. 1967. *Psychological Types. CW,* vol. 6. Princeton, N.J.: Princeton University Press, 1971.

————. 1969. *Memories, Dreams, Reflections.* Aniela Jaffé, ed. Richard and Clara Winston, trans. New York: Vintage, 1989.

————. 1973, 1976. *Letters of C. G. Jung.* 2 vols. Gerhard Adler, ed. New York: Routledge.

————. 1984. *Selected Letters of C. G. Jung, 1909–1961.* Gerhard Adler, ed. in collaboration with Aniela Jaffé. R. F. C. Hull, trans. Princeton, N.J.: Princeton University Press.

Kraft, Kent. 1977. "The Eye Sees More Than the Heart Knows: The

Visionary Cosmology of Hildegard of Bingen." Ph.D. diss., University of Wisconsin.

Labarge, Margaret Wade. 1986. *Women in Medieval Life: A Small Sound of the Trumpet*. London: Hamish Hamilton.

Lachman, Barbara. 1993. *The Journal of Hildegard of Bingen: A Novel*. New York: Bell Tower/Crown Books.

Lammers, Ann Conrad. 1994. *In God's Shadow: The Collaboration of Victor White and C. G. Jung*. New York: Paulist Press.

Lattimore, Richmond, trans. 1951. *The Iliad of Homer*. Chicago: University of Chicago Press.

Leon-Dufour, Xavier. 1987. *Sharing the Eucharistic Bread: The Witness of the New Testament*. Matthew J. O'Connell, trans. New York: Paulist Press.

Lerner, Gerda. 1986. *The Creation of Patriarchy*. New York: Oxford University Press.

———. 1993. *The Creation of Feminist Consciousness: From the Middle Ages to 1870*. New York: Oxford University Press.

———. 1997. *Why History Matters: Life and Thought*. New York: Oxford University Press.

Macy, Gary. 2006. Heloise, Abelard and the ordination of abbesses. *Journal of Ecclesiastical History* 57(1):16–32.

———. 2008. *The Hidden History of Women's Ordination: Female Clergy in the Medieval West*. New York: Oxford University Press.

Maddocks, Fiona. 2001. *Hildegard of Bingen: The Woman of Her Age*. New York: Image Books/Doubleday.

May, Gerald G. 2004. *The Dark Night of the Soul*. San Francisco: HarperCollins.

McDonagh, Séan. 1986. *To Care for the Earth: A Call to a New Theology*. Santa Fe: Bear and Company.

McGinn, Bernard. 1998. *The Flowering of Mysticism: Men and Women in the New Mysticism, 1200–1350*. *The Presence of God: A History of Western Christian Mysticism*, vol. 3. New York: Crossroad Publishing Company.

McGrath, Sister Albertus Magnus, OP. 1971. Woman as the 'niggers' of the Church. *The Critic* (September-October 1971): 24–33.

McInerney, Maud Burnett, ed. 1998. *Hildegard of Bingen: A Book of Essays*. New York: Garland Publishing, Inc.

McNamara, Jo Ann Kay. 1996. *Sisters in Arms: Catholic Nuns Through Two Millennia*. Cambridge, Mass.: Harvard University Press.

Metz, Johann Baptist. 1972. The future in the memory of suffering. *Concilium* 76:15.

Mews, Constant. 2004. "Encountering Hildegard: Between Apocalypse and the New Age." In Louise D'Arcens and Juanita Feros Ruys, eds., *Maistresse of My Wit: Medieval Women, Modern Scholars, Making the Middle Ages*, vol. 7. Turnout, Belgium: Brepols Publishers

Moore, Robert L. 2003. *Facing the Dragon: Confronting Personal and Spiritual Grandiosity.* Wilmette, Ill.: Chiron Publications.

Moore, Thomas. 2004. *Dark Nights of the Soul.* New York: Gotham Books.

Newman, Barbara. 1985. Hildegard of Bingen: Visions and validation. *Church History* 54:163–175.

———. 1987. *Sister of Wisdom: St. Hildegard's Theology of the Feminine.* Berkeley: University of California Press.

———. 1995. *From Virile Woman to WomanChrist: Studies in Medieval Religion and Literature.* Philadelphia: University of Pennsylvania Press.

———. 2000. Uppity trumpet of the Living Light. *London Review of Books* 22(2):19–21.

———. 2003. *Gods and the Goddesses: Vision, Poetry and Belief in the Middle Ages.* Philadelphia: University of Pennsylvania Press.

Newman, Barbara, ed. 1998. *Voice of the Living Light: Hildegard of Bingen and Her World.* Berkeley: University of California Press.

Norris, Kathleen. 2008. *Acedia and Me: A Marriage, Monks, and a Writer's Life.* New York: Riverhead Books.

Oden, Amy, ed. 1994. *In Her Words: Women's Writings in the History of Christian Thought.* Nashville: Abingdon Press.

Ohanneson, Joan. 1997. *Scarlet Music: Hildegard of Bingen.* New York: Crosssroad Publishing Company.

Oliver, Mary. 2006. *Thirst: Poems by Mary Oliver.* Boston: Beacon Press.

O'Shea, Samara. 2008. *Note to Self: On Keeping a Journal and Other Dangerous Pursuits.* New York: HarperCollins.

Otto, Rudolph. 1923. *The Idea of the Holy.* John W. Harvey, trans. London: Oxford University Press.

Pacht, Otto. 1984. *Book Illumination in the Middle Ages: An Introduction.* New York: Oxford University Press.

Pernoud, Régine. 1998. *Hildegard of Bingen: Inspired Conscience of the Twelfth Century.* New York: Marlowe and Company.

Petroff, Elizabeth A., ed. 1986. *Medieval Women's Visionary Literature.* New York: Oxford University Press.

Plaut, W. G. 1981. *The Torah: A Modern Commentary.* New York: Union of American Hebrew Congregations.

Rahner, Karl, SJ. 1971. *Theological Investigations,* vol. 7. London: Darton, Longman and Todd.

———. 1977. "Rahner: Women Priests." *National Catholic Reporter,* October 7, p. 14.

———. 2004. *Karl Rahner: Spiritual Writings.* Philip Endean, ed. Maryknoll, N.Y.: Orbis Press.

Rhodes, Richard. 1995. *How to Write: Advice and Reflections.* New York: HarperCollins.

Richo, David. 2007. *Mary Within Us: A Jungian Contemplation of Her Titles and Powers.* Berkeley, Calif.: Human Development Books.

Rilke, Rainer Maria. 1984. *Letters to a Young Poet.* Stephen Mitchell, trans. New York: Random House.

Ruether, Rosemary Radford. 1991. "The Task of Feminist Theology." In *Doing Theology in Today's World,* John D. Woodbridge and Thomas Edward McComisky, eds. Grand Rapids, Mich.: Zondervan.

————. 1992. *Gaia and God: An Ecofeminist Theology of Earth Healing.* New York: HarperCollins.

Russell, Kenneth. 1989. Matthew Fox's *Illuminations of Hildegard of Bingen. Listening: Journal of Religion and Culture* 24:69–88.

————. 1988. "Patriarchy and Female Invisibility." Presentation made at Mundelein College, Chicago.

Russell, Peter. 1998. *Waking Up in Time: Finding Inner Peace in Times of Accelerating Change.* 10th Anniversary Edition. Navato, Calif.: Origin Press, 2008.

Sacks, Oliver. 1985. *Migraine: Understanding a Common Disorder.* Berkeley: University of California Press.

Sautman, Francesa Canadé, and Pamela Sheingorn, eds. 2001. *Same Sex Love and Desire Among Women in the Middle Ages.* New York: Palgrave.

Sayers, Janet. 2003. *Divine Therapy: Love, Mysticism and Psychoanalysis.* New York: Oxford University Press.

Schipperges, Heinrich. 1997. *Hildegard of Bingen: Healing and the Nature of the Cosmos.* Princeton, N.J.: Markus Wiener Publishers.

Schmitt, Miriam. 1989. St. Hildegard of Bingen: Leaven of God's justice. *Cistercian Studies* 24(1):69–88.

Schneiders, Sandra. 1990. God is more than two men and a bird. *U.S. Catholic* 55(May 5):20–27.

Scholtz, Bernard W. 1980. Hildegard von Bingen on the nature of women." *American Benedictine Review* 31:361–83.

Schroeder-Sheker, Therese. 2001. *Transitus: A Blessed Death in the Modern World.* Missoula, Mont.: St. Dunstan's Press.

Silvas, Anna. 1998. *Jutta and Hildegard: The Biographical Sources.* University Park: Pennsylvania State University Press.

Singer, Charles. 1928. *From Magic to Science: Essays on the Scientific Twilight.* New York: Boni and Liveright.

————. 1917. The scientific views and visions of Saint Hildegard. *Studies in the History and Method of Science* 1:1–55.

Skelton, Ross, general ed. 2006. *The Edinburgh International Encyclopaedia of Psychoanalysis.* Edinburgh: Edinburgh University Press Ltd.

Smith, David. 2007. *If the World Were a Village.* Tonawanda, N.Y.: Kids Can Press Ltd.

Smith, John Maynard. 1998. The origin of altruism. *Nature* 393:639–40.

Stein, Murray. 1985. *Jung's Treatment of Christianity.* Wilmette, Ill.: Chiron Publications.

————. 1996. *Practicing Wholeness.* New York: Continuum.

————. 1998. *Jung's Map of the Soul: An Introduction*. Peru, Ill.: Open Court Press.

Stein, Murray, ed. 1996. *Jung on Evil*. Princeton, N.J.: Princeton University Press.

Strehlow, Wighard. 2002. *Hildegard of Bingen's Spiritual Remedies*. Rochester, Vt.: Healing Arts Press.

Strehlow, Wighard, and Gottfried Hertzka. 1988. *Hildegard of Bingen's Medicine*. Santa Fe: Bear and Company.

Sur, Carolyn Worman. 1993. *The Feminine Images of God in the Visions of Saint Hildegard of Bingen's Scivias*. New York: The Mellen Press.

Sweet, Victoria. 2006. *Rooted in the Earth, Rooted in the Sky: Hildegard of Bingen and Premodern Medicine*. New York: Routledge/Taylor and Francis.

Teilhard de Chardin, Pierre. 1960. *The Divine Milieu*. New York: HarperCollins.

Thompson, Augustine. 1994. Hildegard of Bingen on gender and the Priesthood. *Church History* 63, 111:349–364.

Tillich, Paul. 1948. "You Are Accepted." In *The Shaking of the Foundations*. New York: Charles Scribner.

Turpin, Joanne. 1990. *Women in Church History: Twenty Stories for Twenty Centuries*. Cincinnati: St. Anthony Messenger Press.

Uhlein, Gabriele. 1983. *Meditations with Hildegard of Bingen*. Rochester, Vt.: Bear and Company.

Ulanov, Ann Belford. 1999. *Religion and the Spiritual in Carl Jung*. New York: Paulist Press.

Ulrich, Ingeborg. 1993. *Hildegard of Bingen: Mystic, Healer, Companion of the Angels*. Linda M. Maloney, trans. Collegeville, Minn: The Liturgical Press.

Van de Weyer, Robert, ed. 1997. *Hildegard in a Nutshell*. London: Hodder Headline.

van der Post, Laurent. 1975. *Jung and the Story of Our Time*. New York: Pantheon.

Von Der Heydt, Vera. 1976. *Prospects for the Soul: Soundings in Jungian Psychology and Religion*. London: Darton, Longman and Todd.

Wheatley, Margaret J. 2002. *Turning to One Another: Simple Conversations to Restore Hope to the Future*. San Francisco: Berrett-Koehler Publishers, Inc.

Wheelwright, Jane Hollister. 1984. *For Women Growing Older: The Animus*. Houston: The C. G. Jung Educational Center.

Wiethaus, Ulrike, ed. 1993. *Maps of Flesh and Light: The Religious Experience of Medieval Woman Mystics*. Syracuse, N.Y.: Syracuse University Press.

Wilson, Bill. 1987. *Spiritus contra Spiritum*: The Bill Wilson/C. G. Jung letters: The roots of the Society of Alcoholics Anonymous. *Parabola* 12(2):68–69.

Woodman, Marion. 1987. Worshipping Illusions. *Parabola* 12(2):65.

Yunt, Jeremy D. 2001. Jung's contribution to an ecological psychology. *Journal of Humanistic Psychology* 41(2):96–121.

Zagano, Phyllis. 2000. *Holy Saturday: An Argument for the Restoration of the Female Deaconate in the Catholic Church*. New York: Crossroad Publishing Company.

Index

Avis Clendenen (Ph.D. and D.Min., Chicago Theological Seminary) is the Sister Irene Dugan Scholar in Spirituality and professor of religious studies at Saint Xavier University in Chicago, where she teaches courses in pastoral theology and in the intersections of spirituality and depth psychology. She is coauthor, with Sister Irene Dugan, r.c., of *Love Is All Around in Disguise: Meditations for Spiritual Seekers* (Chiron Publications, 2004); editor of *Spirituality in Depth: Essays in Honor of Sister Irene Dugan, r.c.* (Chiron Publications, 2002); and coauthor, with Troy W. Martin, of *Forgiveness: Finding Freedom Through Reconciliation* (Crossroad Publications, 2002). She can be reached at Clendenen@sxu.edu.